BARBECUED RIBS and Other Great Feeds

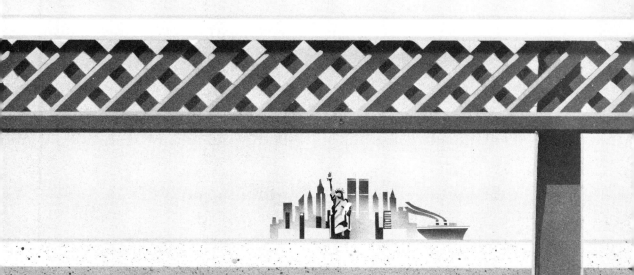

BARBECUED RIBS and Other Great Feeds

BY JEANNE VOLTZ

ALFRED A. KNOPF, NEW YORK, 1987

***This is a Borzoi Book
published by Alfred A. Knopf, Inc.***

Copyright © 1985 by Jeanne Voltz

Library of Congress Cataloging in
Publication Data
Voltz, Jeanne.
Barbecued ribs and other great feeds.
Includes index.
1. Barbecue cookery   I. Title
TX840.B3V63   1985   641.5′784   84-48668
ISBN 0-394 73487-4

Manufactured in
the United States of America
Published April 11, 1985
Second Printing, September 1987

Photo Credits

v, 113: Ray Fisher, The Miami *Herald*
ii. Tony Garnet, The Miami *Herald*
10, 11, 12: Keith Goddard, Works
37: Steve March
192, Carmen Miranda in "The Gang's All
Here": The Museum of Modern Art
vi, 28, 80, 142: Peter Papademetriou

For Luther Jr. and Jeanne Marie, who happily shared
our barbecue experiments

CONTENTS

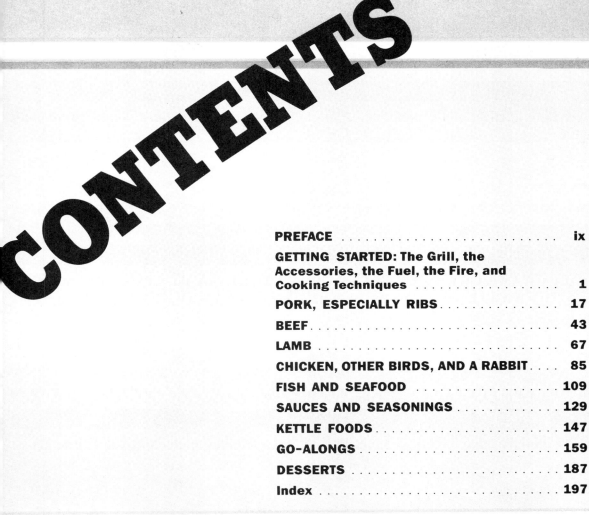

PREFACE

My memory is filled with eating and cooking occasions, and none excites me more than barbecue. To me barbecuing is a celebration of cooking for the pure joy of it and of the savory good food produced by this method of cooking.

You have to love the smell of wood smoke, tangy sauces, and grilling meats. Why else forsake the convenience of a push-button range that holds a perfect temperature for the vagaries of a wood or charcoal fire?

The taste of barbecue is part of my gastronomic heritage. One of my earliest memories is of venison steak sizzling furiously as Daisy, my grandmother's cook, seared it with a great clatter of fork and lid-lifter against the black iron stove. Salt pork bits were sprinkled on the almost red-hot stove lid to fry out and moisten the deer meat, trimmed of most of its own fat. The salt pork melted to send a tantalizing smell forth off the wood fire. The massive black stove is long since gone and venison is not easy to obtain (except for the few times that I can buy it in my favorite butcher shop), but that delicious memory comes to me each time I grill a beef steak and the juices start to sizzle and smell like barbecue.

I was a small girl when I had my first taste of Brunswick stew and first smelled the aroma of pit-roasted pork at a political barbecue, a memory that still makes me hungry today. From mid-childhood through my teens, "weenie" roasts at Big Springs, the water reservoir park in our small town in Alabama, were popular diversions. My mother was horrified to hear that I ate seven hot dogs at the junior high school literary society picnic. I don't remember whether the hot dogs were so good or my conspicuous gluttony was a childish ploy for attention, but I still like hot dogs grilled over charcoal or wood coals.

Later, summer social activity centered around fish fries and the Fourth of July picnic, when an amateur chef would barbecue ribs. The first time I had hushpuppies, the recipe had been brought back from the Gulf Coast. A friend was celebrating a successful fishing trip by inviting twenty or thirty of us to a fish fry, and his wife fried the hushpuppies. Forever after, I fry hushpuppies any time I fry fish. In the South today these crispy onion corn cakes have become traditional with ribs and any kind of barbecued food.

In the winters when I was a child, a farmer in Dry Valley, a few miles from our home, would barbecue goat. On what seemed the coldest day of the year, Mr. Peat would peddle his barbecued goat, driving from house to house in a pick-up truck loaded with trays of the peppered meat. My mother, hearing his bell, would bundle up in her coat and scarf and run to the street to buy a couple of pounds of barbecued goat. That evening Mother would reheat the meat in a covered pan in the oven and serve it with baked sweet potatoes, turnip or collard greens, and hot corn sticks. The meat was deeply smoke flavored (finished in a smokehouse, perhaps) and liberally rubbed with paprika and other spices.

As I grew into young womanhood, dates often ended with a sandwich at Ollie's Barbecue in Birmingham. Other times we would order barbecue at Twin Oaks, a highway stop with two towering oaks that gave it its name. Twin Oaks was demolished to make way for a highway interchange, but the memory of the thick slices of meat awash in spicy-sweet sauce lives on. Ollie's still stands in Birmingham and a friend in New York who grew up there keeps a jar of Ollie's barbecue sauce to spice up leftover beef and pork.

My father enjoyed "weenie" roasts and Fourth of July ribs and would stop for barbecue sandwiches occasionally. He savored Mr. Peat's barbecued kid, comparing one winter's product to that of other years. But Daddy wasn't much of a barbecue cook. Even after patio barbecue fever struck in the fifties and Mother bought a grill, he was a reluctant outdoor chef.

So I was ill-prepared to play admiring wife to a man who became a barbecue fanatic. Tasting, cooking, and discussing good food were absorbing mutual interests of Luther's and mine before and after we were married. Almost before I knew it, he was a weekend chef and I, a semiassistant. One of our first purchases, before we had decent furniture, was a simple barbecue grill.

We began modestly with hot dogs and hamburgers (a common beginner's error, since hamburgers are tricky for the inexperienced). Soon we were barbecuing ribs, chicken, steaks, lamb, and fish. We bought fresh lobster tails at the dock and grilled them, learning the tricks of fire building and heat control as we went along. In no time we were into skewer cookery. Luther's most ambitious company supper became kebabs that combined beef, lamb, calf's liver, sometimes lamb's kidneys with bacon squares, and fresh vegetables. I would busily marinate pounds of meat and then help thread the skewers. And I was often asked to test the doneness of the food and sometimes to baste and turn a grilling chicken or steak.

Early on we settled that a woman can barbecue as well as a man, and in my opinion what a woman lacks in showmanship is made up for in a feel for details such as discreet use of basting sauce and sensing just the right stage of doneness. But if two of you cook, you'll disagree at times and when friends enter the arena the quibbles become hilarious. Luther and I, through thirty years of marriage and barbecuing, never came to a meeting of the minds on how long to cook food. He liked ribs and chicken dark brown, crisp, and dry. I prefer them juicy and golden.

In the years of cooking together we dug mussels in the sand at Lake Tavares in central Florida when the egrets and we were the only mussel eaters. Local folk said they were poisonous, but we enjoyed them in health, though they were a bit chewy. We grilled freshly caught sunfish no bigger than my outstretched palm and served them with grits and bacon as breakfasts and suppers.

We barbecued hundreds of chickens basted with a sauce prescribed by John Wahl. John, an attorney in Miami, grew up in north Florida, so we called it Jacksonville barbecue sauce. We passed the recipe along to barbecue chefs in the family and when our daughter was living in London she once telephoned overseas for Dad's barbecue sauce recipe. Luther's adaptation is on page 21 and still is my favorite for chicken, ribs, and other pork.

On our grills went almost any cut of pork, beef, and lamb, as well as

veal, turkey, once a guinea hen, and even coot. However, the coot was so stringy and fishy flavored that we decided it was not worth the effort.

When we moved to California in the sixties, our barbecuing took on an Oriental flavor. Luther started grilling beef Korean style and barbecuing steaks with teriyaki-like sauces. We experimented with Polynesian-style cookery and California friends inspired us to refine our methods of barbecuing ribs and roast pork Chinese fashion.

We took to early California-style barbecue with enthusiasm, grilling enormous steaks and serving them with salsa, the fresh tomato and chile sauce, and rib-sticking beans and sourdough bread. Historically, ranch barbecues were born of a need for social life in a sparsely settled land. Until this century, guests would arrive from long distances by horseback and stay several days. The hosts would slaughter a steer and barbecue it, cook huge pots of chili beans, and mix the salsa of fresh tomatoes and other available vegetables, foods that still distinguish California barbecues.

In the summer, our daily routine was to put meat or chicken to marinate before we went to work, then grill it after a swim when we came home. In the winters, we often set the hibachi in the fireplace to grill steak, fish, or lamb quickly after work. Through the years we patronized barbecue cafes, and Luther never thought his ribs quite came up to those barbecued by the churchwomen of Coconut Grove, Florida. The women would cook the ribs slowly over small fires built in battered washtubs. They basted them with sauces that defy analysis and will forever be secret. The ribs were sharp with lime juice, slightly sweet and tangy, but those women were tight-lipped about the details. Lunch at Shorty's, down Dixie Highway toward Key West, was another treat. We sat at benches arranged family style, your bench mate often a traveler en route to or from the airport. I marveled at how the furs and topcoats ready for the trip north escaped drips of barbecue sauce and drooling butter from the corn.

Our children were just toddlers when they learned to spot a barbecue stand a mile down a highway by the smoke floating over it. Smoke sometimes is for show only, the meat being roasted in an oven and brushed with sauce. I've found no sure way to locate good barbecue on the road, even in prime barbecue country. I've often asked service station attendants, and once got a great tip from an ice platform boss in north Florida; supermarket check-out clerks can be reliable sources of information if you find a friendly one. Some suggestions from home folk have been good, some not. I blame this on individual taste and local pride in neon and chrome, more than food.

The recent rage for barbecue cafes in New York and other cities pleases me mightily. Hardly any bought barbecue is the same as one made at home or cooked by an expert in a country churchyard, but I can walk to three places from my apartment in the heart of the city to buy ribs, and one of them is very good.

Nonetheless, I still barbecue joyfully. My husband died in the seventies and the last meal we shared was barbecued ribs cooked at the little house in Coconut Grove that we had bought for vacations. Now I light a fire in a short-legged grill on my New York apartment terrace. This tiny grill accommodates food for four or six easily, a whole butterflied leg of lamb, a beef tenderloin, ribs, and chicken.

Barbecuing is convivial cooking. No outdoor sport invites more kibitzers, whether you're in Florida, California, New York City, or a roadside stop in Kansas. I've had hundreds of advisers, from amateurs to men and women who make a precise science of barbecue cooking. I still find slips of paper on which Luther, in his journalistic shorthand, wrote: "2½ lb. ribs, 10 min., turn, 1½ hr., 2 pts. sauce."

The results of a lifetime of eating and testing over smoky fires are all here in this book. I'm grateful to have collaborated with an opinionated chef, Luther, and our two children, who took pleasure in trying new foods. Now, never again must I hunt for a scrap of paper on which I wrote, "chicken, 10 minutes on one side, turn and baste—." It's here, for all of us to enjoy!

GETTING STARTED

Unpacking a new grill, affixing the legs with the bolts and nuts provided, if the grill came unassembled, and grilling the first steak or frankfurter is a big thrill. But it is not quite that easy! Superb food depends on your developing skills at the grill. First, read the instructions that come with the grill. These may consist of a few sentences on the carton or a detailed manual. A manual can be your bible as you use and care for your grill during its lifetime, so put the manual away with the instructions for use of other household equipment. It will be there when you run into an unexpected problem like a balky fire that won't sear meat. The manual should also give advice on storing your grill and cleaning it so that it will last a long time and look attractive.

As you become experienced, you will work out cooking and fire-tending techniques to produce food to meet your standards. First, choose a grill to suit your cooking needs and the space that is available to it—back yard, patio, miniature garden, city apartment terrace, or picnic park.

THE GRILL

Some of the best barbecued chicken I've had was cooked on an old oven rack set precariously on two small stacks of bricks with the fire burning between the bricks. Elaborate equipment is not necessary to successful barbecuing, but a well-designed grill makes barbecuing easier and more efficient.

The price of a serviceable grill ranges from $12 to $15 for a small simple brazier to $200 or $300 for a grill with gadgets and attachments. There are four types of grills.

The first kind is a brazier, or hibachi—basically a tray or pan to hold the fire with a grill on top of it. Small braziers are portable and so especially useful for picnics. The simplest open braziers have no vents or dampers to help you control heat and usually the distance between fire and grill cannot be adjusted, but many good foods such as steaks and frankfurters can be cooked on them.

The second type is a grill with hood. This is a brazier or firepot with a metal baffle or hood that shields the cooking surface and fire from the elements. On a windy day, a hood that can be turned to shut off the wind can be very useful.

A third sort is a covered grill—a brazier or firepot with a cover that goes in place after you start the fire or start cooking. The cover holds in heat and shuts off enough air to discourage flare-ups. Round grills with rounded covers are called barbecue kettles and look like giant kettles standing on a base. Rectangular grills with covers and on wheels are sometimes called grill wagons, since they move around somewhat like pushcarts. The heat control provided by a cover with properly placed dampers and vents makes a covered grill worthwhile to a serious barbecue chef. The cover also holds in smoke to capture the maximum benefit from smoldering wood and herbs.

A fourth variety of grill is known as a water smoker. This is a modern adaptation of an ancient Chinese smoke oven. The firebox is low in a deep kettle-type grill, a pan of water is positioned about halfway up the grill chamber, and the grill, near the top. This mode of cooking produces an intense smoky flavor but does not grill meat brown and crusty like a conventional grill. However, most water smokers can be used without the water pan for dry grilling.

Gas or electric grills for the deck or back yard appeal to barbecue cooks who want a fire to burn when and how they need it. These grills come in a wide variety of sizes and shapes. They are equipped with a ceramic plate or other device in the firebox to catch drippings and heat them so they sizzle and create good cooking odors. The effect is not quite like charcoal or wood fire smoke, but cooking this way is foolproof—just plug in the grill or light the gas—and the grills are easy to clean.

A gas grill that is hot enough to grill steaks and sear meats quickly usually provides 80 to 110 BTUs per square inch of grill surface. Check this feature if you expect to see steaks take on a deep burnished color quickly. The smaller, less expensive and less sturdy grills are ideal for camping, when your main cooking may be heating up canned staples or cooking fish, which requires lower heat than meat. But you need to have one of the larger solid grills made by a good manufacturer for fast effective searing. The top-of-the-line grill in one line provides 108,000 BTUs whereas the small portable grills put out only 24,000 to 40,000 BTUs, which may be good for hot dogs or hamburgers, but too slow for a thick steak.

Several manufacturers (Jenn-Air was among the first) produce countertop grills similar to the equipment used in restaurant kitchens. The grills are powered by gas or electricity and have a unique venting system which causes the fumes to be absorbed at the cooking center. Meat cooked on a countertop grill of this type has a rich flavor, but not quite like real outdoor cooking to my taste. However, after my brother installed this type of grill in his home in San Francisco he almost never cooked meat except on the grill, and I enjoyed many steaks, slabs of country ham, and breakfast sausages from it.

Shop for a grill with a sturdy base or wheeled carriage to make it tip-proof. A spit, often an optional extra at added cost, is worthwhile if you plan to barbecue large pieces of meat and birds. Good spits can be purchased separately, too. If you are really into serious cooking, a firebox or grill that can be cranked up or down is invaluable in keeping heat at just the level you want it.

Other attachments are optional: shelves at the rim of the grill, hooks for hanging tools, racks for roasts or corn. I prefer a separate worktable or cart to hold the sauce, tongs, and other gear. The silliest attachment, or so I thought, was a grill with its own umbrella . . . until the night my husband held the household umbrella over the fire to finish a big batch of shish kebab during a sudden rainstorm.

THE ACCESSORIES

Barbecue accessories can clutter your toolshed if you let friends bring you every wild gadget they see or if you fall for funny aprons and artsy-craftsy tools. Following are what I feel to be the essentials.

Long-handled tongs, fork, and pancake turner (to turn meats and vegetables, not usually pancakes).

Mitts made of heavy-duty and nonflammable material. Welders' gloves work well, but more attractive barbecue mitts are serviceable, too.

A water spritzer or something to squirt a thin stream of water on a burst of flame. My favorite is a toy water pistol, but spritzer bottles such as those used for window cleaning or misting plants, or a soft drink bottle that you squirt from by holding your finger half over the bottle mouth, work well, too.

One or more basting brushes—a long-handled brush, a fine-bristled paintbrush kept for this purpose, or a dish mop (the kind you find in variety stores). Basting brushes should of course be washed between uses.

A drip pan to set among the coals for large roasts and ribs. I use a shallow baking pan wrapped inside and out with heavy-duty aluminum foil to save scouring afterward. Disposable foil pans are handy, too.

One or two saucepans and skillets for sauces and grill-top sautéing. I use kitchen cookware, protected with foil wrappers.

A fire starter—an electric one to place among briquets to get them going fast, or a chimney-type device in which you build a small fire to put in the coals to start them.

The gas-station smell of liquid fire starter taints food, so if you use it make sure that every trace of the lingering aroma has burned away before you put food on the fire. Use liquid fire starter sparingly and burn it at least 45 minutes before putting food on the fire (see page 12).

Aprons, hot-pot lifters, and a poker or fireplace shovel to push around coals are aids to good barbecuing. I like an apron with a towel hanging at the waist, since I am a constant hand wiper.

Other equipment is useful, but optional.

A hinged wire grill that opens like a book, then locks closed to hold foods that tend to crumble or stick to the grill. This is especially helpful for handling hamburgers, fish, small steaks, chops, and a batch of chicken legs or wings.

A set of good skewers, for vegetables and small shellfish, as well as shish kebab. Flat blades twisted into an elongated corkscrew shape hold food firmly. Wood skewers must be soaked in water or have a piece of carrot pushed on the end to prevent burning. Metal skewers should have handles easily grasped with your hands in gloves or heat-resistant handles that stay cool.

Racks for corn, potatoes, and other small foods help organize space on a crowded grill and allow circulation of heat. Roast racks hold a piece of meat steady and tumble baskets that are attached to a spit rod eliminate the need to turn cut ribs or chicken pieces.

An instant-registering thermometer is essential for judging the doneness of large pieces of meat. Keep it in the apron pocket.

You'll use lots of aluminum foil, paper towels and napkins, and waxed paper on which to place a messy brush before you wash it.

THE FUEL

Charcoal briquets or wood charcoal remain the standard fuel for outdoor cooking, in spite of the rage for mesquite, fruit and nut woods, and other fire makers, but if you lose a tree to storm or disease—an oak, hickory, or other nonresinous wood—by all means have it cut to burn in your grill.

Wood charcoal is simply that—wood burned in an oven to dry it and make it burn with more intense heat than raw dry wood. It is rather porous, so it is easy to ignite and burns down quickly.

Charcoal briquets are sawdust or fine wood chips or other pulpy material dried in an oven and compressed into neat squares; hence the name briquets. They vary widely in quality. Some burn hotter than others, some burn longer, some start more easily, and some smell woodsy and alluring when burning. Others have a crankcase-like smell due to excessive use of petroleum mastic to hold the pulp together. The worst that I have used were a pulpy material, something like shredded corrugated cardboard, pressed together in an oily substance. These were manufactured in the South one year, but fortunately the manufacturer has moved off to Australia and taken his charcoal with him. I'm sure others just as bad are around.

As some of the best and worst briquets are regionally available, a beginning barbecue chef must do his own testing and selecting. I've had help from hardware store salesmen who swore by this or that briquet, and sometimes I disagree with their choices. Friends talk charcoal over back fences too, so listen and learn what you can.

Unfortunately, charcoal briquets have no standard of identity. Briquets are labeled "compressed wood charcoal," with no mention of the mastic. Some charcoal is compressed mechanically with a minimum of mastic that is almost odorless. Others are glued together with smelly petroleum by-products. Reputable oil companies that produce charcoal briquets label the oil ingredient and generally formulate briquets so that the oil odor burns off before the fire is ready for cooking.

Smell charcoal before you buy it; sniff a torn bag if you find one. Briquets that smell very strongly of motor oil may not cook away this smell to release fresh woodsy aromas. Heavily oily briquets have a greasy feel and leave black smudges on your hands. Good-quality compressed wood chips leave a powdery film on your hands, almost as light as the charcoal used in artwork. The compressed wood briquets have a clean, slight burnt-wood smell, perhaps with a faint scent of kindling resins.

Each time we moved we would select charcoal anew, due to the lack of national brands and the abundance of good regional brands. I would buy a small bag (two pounds) of each of the likely-looking charcoals and try them one by one. When I found the one that suited me best, I would buy a 10- or 25-pound bag of it and stick with it until something better appeared in the stores.

The tradition of special woods for special foods goes back hundreds of years. When the white man first came to the Pacific Northwest, Indians were grilling salmon over alderwood fires, and outdoor cooks in Washington State still use alder for salmon. In France small sweet-meated fish and quick-cooking meats are grilled over dried grapevine cuttings, and sea bass is grilled over fires of dried fennel stalks. In Sweden I once had smoked salmon heated on a bed of fir rinsed in the Baltic Sea to prevent it from flaming up on the grill. The slightly warmed salmon was served with a mustard and dill sauce, boiled potatoes, and sliced fresh cucumbers and dill. The smoky, slightly resinous flavor in the salmon was a delectable surprise.

Mesquite, which grows like a weed in the Southwest from Texas to California, is the wood of the moment. Restaurants from New York to Honolulu advertise that their fish is grilled over mesquite. However, Betsey Balsley, food editor of the Los Angeles *Times*, told me in the spring of 1984 that mesquite is in short supply, not because there isn't enough of it, but because not enough of it is harvested among the Joshua trees and other stickery cactus where it grows. Betsey thinks that restaurants touting mesquite barbecue use only a few chips on the fire to provide aroma.

The chief advantage of mesquite, if you fall heir to a chunk or a bag of charcoal, is a hot fire, which sears the food quickly. Mesquite imparts a lightly woody flavor—best on beef, good on poultry, but sometimes slightly bitter on fish, so I use a few chips rather than a mesquite fire for fish. Hickory provides an intense smoky aroma, the preferred flavor for barbecued ribs, poultry, and beef. Other nut woods such as pecan or walnut also give off a fine smoky aroma that perks up almost any meat. However, if you let a hickory fire burst into flame, it leaves an unattractive sooty residue on meat.

Apple and cherry wood chips or chunks provide a fruity smoke and are especially good on chicken, turkey, pork, and smoked meats such as ham and sausages. In New England apple-wood smoked turkey is an autumn tradition. Apple wood gives meat a faint golden color and cherry wood turns food a reddish brown.

Twigs or small branches cut from trees or shrubs in your garden can be used to flavor grilled meats. Be sure the wood is nonpoisonous (no oleander, please!) and nonresinous (no pine or fir) and that the twigs and foliage have not been sprayed recently with pesticides.

Kindling sticks are the important exception to nonresinous woods. They come in gift packs now and are used to start a wood or charcoal fire. But these should not be added in the last stages of smoking, unless you like a bitter piney flavor.

The customary smoking wood in south Florida is Australian pine—not a true pine but the casuarina tree, found in most back yards. Because it grows so profusely it needs frequent pruning. We would clip a few feathery branch tips, soak them in water, and put them on the barbecue fire 10 or 15 minutes before chicken or pork was done. The smoky flavor was better than hickory, a guest said one evening.

Wood fragrance makers come in several forms—small logs or hunks to serve as the main part of the fire, sticks or small chunks to be added to the fire for aroma about 15 minutes before you finish cooking, and chips, to be soaked in water and sprinkled on a hot fire 10 minutes before cooking is over. Chips are the most efficient way of using wood and generally provide as much exotic smoke flavor as you want.

THE FIRE

Building a good fire and keeping it that way defeat many stout-hearted barbecue cooks, so don't despair if you have a few false starts before you master fire building. Start the fire 30 to 45 minutes before cooking to allow it to burn down to glowing hot coals. Tossing food on the fire before it is ready produces blackened but half-raw meat. The other common error of fire building is using too much charcoal. Not only is excessive charcoal wasteful, it fuels a fire so fiercely that food is burned to a black ghost of itself and dried out beyond good eating quality.

Before you start the fire, clean away any ashes left from the last cooking, as ashes block air circulation to the fire. Adjust dampers and vents for maximum ventilation to start the fire, and turn a grill or hood to catch the best breeze. However, when the breeze is strong, shield the fire from heavy wind by turning the grill or positioning the hood or baffle to block the wind.

If a grill has no vents and dampers, set it strategically to catch the best breeze for starting the fire and if the air is very still and the fire balky, you might pep up the blaze with a fireplace bellows or fan the fire vigorously with a folded newspaper to get it burning. After the fire is started a grill that has no vents can be shielded from too much draft with a sheet of plywood or other screen. Anything will do — we once rigged up a child's blackboard to protect the fire from wind.

Lay the fire loosely in the firebox. Some barbecue cooks like to line the firebox with aluminum foil to reflect and intensify heat slightly, and a lining of foil certainly helps with clean-up, but I like the look of glowing coals against the dark firebox. First crumple two or three sheets of newspaper and place them in the bottom of the firebox loosely enough so that

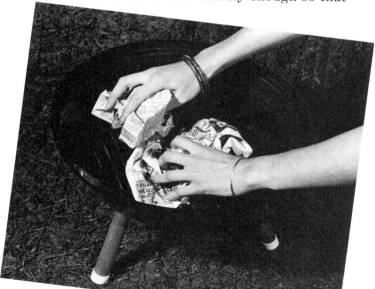

there are air pockets to let flames lick through it freely. Crisscross kindling sticks or twigs over the paper or arrange them in a small teepee shape. I use small pine sticks or other resinous wood or dry twigs for kindling.

An electric fire starter gets a fire going fast. If you use it, place it over the paper and kindling pile. Now arrange 15 to 20 briquets over the fire starter, paper, and kindling, mounding them slightly but allowing plenty of air for easier catching. This size fire is big enough for ribs or chicken if more coals are added during cooking. You need only about 10 briquets for a few hot dogs or a couple of steaks.

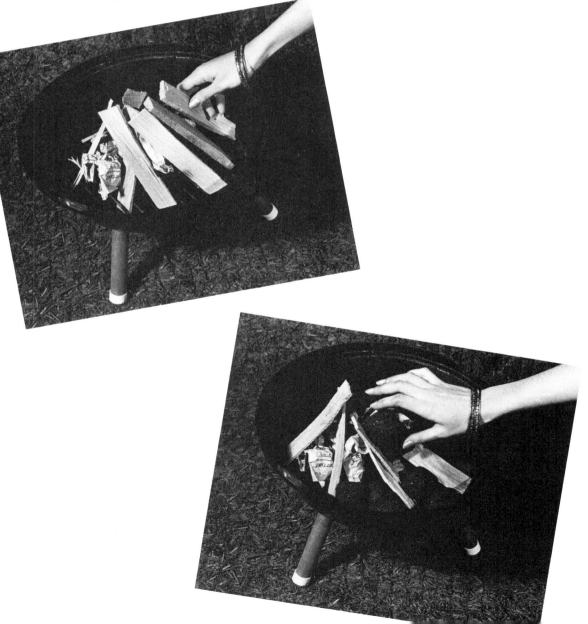

If using, plug in the fire starter, following the manufacturer's directions; or if not, touch a match to two or three corners of the newspaper at the base of the pile.

When the charcoal starts to blaze, in about 10 minutes, remove the fire starter to prevent damaging it. If the fire is burning vigorously, adjust dampers and hood to direct ventilation as needed.

I prefer the electric fire starter to other methods of lighting a charcoal fire. But liquid fire starter can be used successfully if you make sure the fumes burn off before you start cooking. The trick is to soak 2 or 3 briquets in fire starter and put them in the center of the fire, just over the newspaper. The starter-soaked briquets will light the other briquets and the odor burns away before you start cooking (although I have to admit that my imagination lets the smell linger long after it should have burned off). Also, remember a safety rule: never pour liquid starter on a balky fire, as it can leap up dangerously and light the fluid in the can.

Another method of starting a fire is with a device, available in hardware and specialty shops, called a lighter chimney. It is a cylinder about the size of a large tomato juice can with holes in it. You start several briquets burning in it with newspaper as kindling and then turn the minifire out into the grill as the core for your cooking fire.

We once devised a home version of this system. We used a beer can opener to cut four wedges in the sides at the bottom of a coffee can. We put

4 or 5 briquets in our "starter" and set it over a gas flame on the kitchen range. In a few minutes the minifire was ready to be put in the grill and topped with more briquets to build the fire. I warn you, though, that you need very sturdy mitts for this operation to bring the gas-flamed fire from the kitchen to the grill safely.

Once the fire is started you can relax a minute or two, though a good fire has a tendency to go out when you're not looking. My husband used to poke it and stare at it during its entire start-up time. In about 30 to 45 minutes it should be ready for cooking. The fire is perfect when a rosy glow winks between the coals and the tops of the coals are coated with gray-white ash. Spread the coals in the grill, one layer deep—close together for thick steaks, meaty ribs, or chicken; about a half-inch apart for hot dogs, thin steaks, and other quick-cooking foods.

COOKING TECHNIQUES

The proof of a good barbecue cook lies in his or her total immersion in the art of cooking, and enjoying the challenge of getting the fire perfect, food cooked to taste, sauces and seasonings artfully mated to the food. Too much mediocre food gets by because amateur cooks toss it on grills, with little regard for the limitations of cooking the simplest food over a fire in the most basic of cooking equipment.

To understand barbecue cooking, one must realize that the heat is dry, intense, and not easily controlled. Charcoal or wood fires are suitable primarily for prime or choice beef, first-quality tender pork cuts, lamb, and tender poultry. Less tender meats require special handling, marinating, or grinding (as with sausages) to make them edible on a barbecue fire. Thick cuts of meat must be cooked long and slowly to insure thorough heat penetration.

So first, buy top-quality ingredients and the foods best suited to this sort of heat. It makes no sense to skimp on food costs when you must spend a couple of dollars on a bag of charcoal, and much more on wood chips, the grill, and other equipment involved.

Accompanying ingredients—butter, olive and other oils, vinegar, and wines used in cooking—should be of the best quality. This means not necessarily the highest-priced wines, but wines of good flavor to be sure the taste complements the food.

Having acquired fine ingredients, treat them with respect. Barbecuing requires patience, careful watching, and an educated eye, nose, and touch for the doneness of foods.

Meat is seared over a hot charcoal fire, then moved to a less hot area of the grill to continue cooking. Fast-cooking meat such as steak usually is done by the time a good crust cooks on it—at least for rare-meat fans.

Meat that takes longer than 15 minutes to cook benefits from finishing under the cover of a grill or covered by a loose drape of aluminum foil. The foil is tucked loosely around the meat to hold in the heat—not underneath, as that would deter heat penetration. Pull away the foil or cover from time to time, and baste and turn the meat as needed.

A lightweight cover can be constructed of coathanger wires and foil for an open brazier. Bend and fasten the wires into a four-rib umbrella-like frame with a round base and cover it with foil. A vent at the peak of the dome allows heat circulation and serves as a simple damper which you can pinch closed or open wider, according to the needs of the fire or (pinched closed) when you want to intensify smoke flavor. Heat on a grill is controlled by raising or lowering the grill or firebox. If neither grill nor firebox is movable, regulate heat by spreading the coals for a medium heat, pushing them closer together for a hotter fire.

For long-cooking foods, you may need to replenish the fire from time to time with more charcoal briquets. When grilling a turkey or other large piece of meat, I build a fire in a smaller grill set close to the main cooking grill. As more coals are needed, I lift a few with tongs from the auxiliary fire, which keeps the main fire going steadily.

Turn meat as needed to keep dripping fat from blazing and to keep heat even. Don't let the top side of a piece of meat get cold before you turn it to the fire again. About every 10 minutes is sufficient turning for most foods, and half-chickens can be turned only every 20 minutes if you keep the fire low enough to prevent burning. Don't use sauces too often or too heavily. A light brushing with sauce each time you turn meat usually is sufficient. Sauces containing large amounts of oil or other fats, sugar, or tomato should be used very sparingly as they feed the fire and make it jump furiously to char meat. Experienced barbecue cooks use these flammable sauces only in the last 10 to 15 minutes of cooking.

Cooking times are unpredictable due to the variables of wind, fire heat, and chef's diligence. A fuss-budget cook can prolong cooking by basting and turning meat so frequently that it never really heats to cooking temperature. On the other hand, if you let meat stand in one position too long, it overcooks on one side and is half done on the other.

Barbecue is a matter of taste. If you appreciate well-cooked food, you'll soon learn to smell, feel, and taste when barbecue is cooked perfectly. My preference is for meat that is well-browned, crusty and crispy, well-seasoned with sauce, and moist all the way through. Some friends like it dry and crackly all the way through. Each to his own liking, and if you half try, you'll find your way.

PORK, ESPECIALLY RIBS

Barbecued ribs are positively a mania with young America. There are pork barbecue places open all over. A modest French restaurant on my street in New York City closed for renovation and two weeks later opened as a barbecued ribs joint, complete with "sidewalk cafe," a ridiculously tiny square of Astroturf with two tables on it. In the fall of 1983 the *New York Times* reported that a fashion designer noted for her good cooking had invited guests to her Upper East Side apartment for a buffet of ribs and trimmings, the ribs ordered in.

In the Carolinas, Georgia, and Texas, barbecued ribs have always been on family-style restaurant menus or available in specialty restaurants within a mile of almost any highway stop. They are barbecued on the premises. Now in New York, ribs cooked in a smoke oven or cooked in any number of ways are shipped in from New Jersey or as far away as Texas, then sauced and reheated at the restaurant. They're good at many places, but not like home cooking. Barbecuing ribs in your back yard allows you to season ribs to taste from beginning to end of the cooking, and to serve them with a table sauce of your choice.

Carolinians, Georgians, Mississippians, Alabamians, and Floridians would all fight over whose ribs are best. The Chinese of San Francisco, New York, and Boston cook still another style of barbecued ribs. Recipes in this chapter have been adapted from the dozens of pounds of ribs that I have sampled, cooked, and enjoyed throughout my life.

Pork is the preferred meat, practically the only meat, for barbecuing in the Carolinas and is highly favored in Georgia and the Deep South. Pigs were brought from England by the first settlers on the James River in Virginia, and Southerners have been pork lovers ever since. Hispanics now add their flavors to the barbecue choice. On holidays the lusty aroma of barbecuing pig floats through the Cuban districts of Miami, Key West, and Tampa, and I am told that pig is barbecued in the Cuban colonies in New Jersey. Vietnamese, Malaysians, Indonesians, and Thai settlers bring yet another dimension to barbecued pork, and anybody who frequents Chinatowns, U.S.A., knows Chinese barbecued pork in many styles.

Pork is especially good for barbecuing because it absorbs the smoky aroma compatibly and finishes off crispy and chewy over a charcoal fire. An ever-increasing variety of pork cuts is available in markets, thanks to new systems of cutting and packing pork in processing plants. Doubtless pork is chosen for barbecuing because of its flavor, but it has health benefits in its superior supply of vitamin B and high-quality protein with lower fat than some other meats.

BARBECUED RIBS

There are three types of ribs—spareribs, cut from just behind the pork shoulder; back ribs; and country-style ribs, cut from the loin. America's favorites are spareribs, a long triangular cut of bones, cartilage, and a thin layer of meat that grills to a crispiness and flavor like no other food. Back ribs are shorter than spareribs, and so daintier finger food, and are first choice for Chinese-style barbecue. Country-style ribs cut from the loin are nuggets of meat attached to bones. They cook tender and juicy, are meaty, but crispy.

Any kind of ribs can be cooked by the methods here. Recipes for seasoning mixes and sauces are in the sauce chapter. Deciding upon a sauce can start a back yard barbecue battle. A Carolina-style sauce is vinegary and spicy, a Florida-style sauce is perky, flavored and tinged with catsup, and never the twain shall meet.

These are the major cooking methods for home grills.

GRILL AND BASTE, OPEN FIRE

Ribs left in large pieces (a side if they are spareribs) are easier to turn and baste than cut ribs. Cut them in serving pieces after they are cooked. The large size can be crucial when cooking on an open brazier and a fire leaps out of control. The chef needs to work fast with tongs and basting brush to turn the ribs away from the sooty fire—while squirting water on the offending flames.

Raise grill 8 to 10 inches above hot coals, if possible. If grill level cannot be adjusted, build fire carefully so there is no more than one layer of coals and have coals ready to replenish the fire (place them at the edge of the fire and poke them into the center as other coals burn out).

If using a vinegar sauce or bone-broth sauce, brush on ribs. Do not, to start, brush on a sweet sauce, fatty sauce, or one containing a large amount of catsup.

Place ribs on grill over coals that have burned down until covered with ash. Watch carefully and turn each time flames leap up. Baste occasionally with one of the light sauces (see pages 132-3). After 30 minutes, start basting sparingly with one of the sweet sauces such as Georgia Barbecue Sauce, Texas Barbecue Sauce, Orange Peel Barbecue Sauce, and Raisinberry Sauce (see pages 134-9). Continue to turn and baste ribs every 5 to 10 minutes until done—30 to 45 minutes longer. Cut near center and if juices run clear ribs are done. If pink, cook a few minutes longer. Brush again with sauce. Remove to a platter. Cut in 2- and 3-rib portions, using kitchen shears or a sharp knife, and serve with more sauce or a table sauce, if desired.

GRILL AND BASTE, CLOSED GRILL

Place ribs on grill 5 to 6 inches above hot fire. Baste with a vinegar or bone-broth sauce, but not catsup or sweet sauce. Brown on one side; turn, baste, and brown the other. Baste ribs lightly with a sweet sauce, heavily with vinegar or bone-broth sauce, cover grill, and adjust dampers and vents to prevent fire flare-ups. Cook, turning and basting ribs every 10 to 15 minutes, about 45 minutes or until crispy and done.

Uncover grill, brush ribs again with sauce, turn, and grill 2 or 3 minutes. Brush with sauce, turn, and grill 2 or 3 minutes. Remove to a platter, cut in serving pieces, using kitchen shears or a sharp knife. Serve with more sauce or a table sauce, if desired.

TEXAS BARBECUED RIBS

In spite of their noted preference for barbecued beef, Texans barbecue pork ribs on occasion. Their method is among the most elaborate—a seasoning rub on the meat first, a basting sauce, and yet another table sauce to produce rich meaty flavor with the spicy sauce there if you want it.

4 to 5 pounds spareribs
Rib Seasoning Mix (page 131)
Bone-Broth Basting Sauce (page 132)
Texas Barbecue Sauce (page 136)

*Makes
5 to 6
servings.*

Sprinkle ribs generously with seasoning mix, rubbing some of it under the flap of meat on the bony side of each slab. Brush well with bone-broth sauce and place ribs 4 to 5 inches above hot fire on a grill with cover. Brown on one side, baste, and turn. Brown well. Cover grill, adjust dampers so fire burns slowly, and grill ribs until done, about 45 minutes. Turn and baste as needed for even cooking. Remove cover of grill, baste and turn ribs again, and remove to platter. Cut into serving-size sections and serve with Texas Barbecue Sauce and coleslaw.

LUTHER'S BARBECUED RIBS

My husband preferred barbecued ribs to almost any other food, and he must have barbecued two to three thousand pounds of them this way in his lifetime.
The sauce for this recipe circulated first around north Florida, then Miami barbecue grills for years. Luther's rule was limes for ribs, lemon in the sauce for chicken. At various times, we plucked the limes off our back yard tree.

4 to 5 pounds spareribs
Florida Barbecue Sauce (page 135)

*Makes
4 to 6
servings.*

Place ribs about 6 inches above hot coals. Brush lightly with sauce and brown on one side. Keep a water bottle handy when using this sauce as it causes flames to shoot up. Turn, brush again with sauce, and brown the other side. Continue turning and basting about every 10 minutes until ribs are done, about 1 hour. Check by cutting near bone in a center section. If juices run clear or golden the ribs are done. Remove ribs to a platter. Cut into 1- to 3-rib sections with scissors or a sharp knife and serve with any remaining sauce.

BARBECUED RIBS WITH SALSA

4 to 5 pounds country-style ribs
Rib Seasoning Mix (page 131)
1 small onion, chopped
1 clove garlic, minced
1 tablespoon oil
1 (8-ounce) can tomato sauce
2 to 4 tablespoons chopped green chiles (canned or
    roasted fresh)
Salt to taste

Makes

4 to 6

servings.

Sprinkle ribs with seasoning mix and place 4 to 6 inches above hot coals. Grill about 45 minutes, turning as needed to cook evenly and extinguishing any flames with squirts of water.

Meanwhile, in a saucepan over moderate heat cook onion and garlic in oil until tender but not browned. Add tomato sauce and bring to a boil. Remove from heat and add chiles. Taste and add salt, if needed. When ribs are done brush lightly with the sauce (salsa) and cook a minute or two longer. Remove ribs to platter; cut into serving-size sections, using scissors or a sharp knife. Serve salsa on the side.

PEPPERY BARBECUED RIBS

1 medium onion, diced

1 rib celery, diced, to make ½ cup

2 tablespoons oil

2 cloves garlic, minced

1 cup catsup

½ cup water

2 tablespoons cider vinegar

1 teaspoon freshly ground black pepper

1 teaspoon crushed red pepper

4 to 5 pounds country-style ribs

2 teaspoons Rib Seasoning Mix (page 131)

Makes 4 to 6 servings.

In an enamelware or stainless-steel saucepan sauté onion and celery in oil until almost tender. Add garlic and sauté 2 or 3 minutes longer. Add catsup, water, vinegar, and the peppers. Simmer uncovered 15 minutes to blend flavors. Stir occasionally and add more water if sauce thickens too much.

Sprinkle ribs generously with seasoning mix. Grill 4 to 5 inches over hot fire, turning often, until browned and almost done, about 40 minutes. Brush lightly with sauce and turn and grill until browned and done, about 15 minutes longer. Heat and serve remaining sauce with the ribs at table.

GLAZED COUNTRY RIBS

4 to 5 pounds country-style ribs
Rib Seasoning Mix (page 131)
Bone-Broth Basting Sauce (page 132)
2 tablespoons cornstarch
1/4 cup packed brown sugar
1 1/2 cups pineapple juice
1/4 cup prepared horseradish
2 tablespoons cider vinegar
Freshly grated horseradish, if available

Makes
5 to 6
servings.

Rub ribs with seasoning mix. Place on grill 6 to 8 inches above hot coals, brush with bone-broth sauce, and grill until browned. Turn and brown the other side. Continue grilling, turning and basting, until ribs are almost done, about 45 minutes.

Meanwhile, in a small saucepan blend cornstarch and brown sugar. Stir in pineapple juice until smooth. Bring to a boil at edge of grill, stirring constantly, and cook and stir until thickened and clear. Stir in horseradish and vinegar. Keep glaze warm. Brush glaze on ribs and cook and turn until they are shiny. Remove ribs to platter and cut into serving-size sections, using scissors or a sharp knife. Serve remaining glaze with ribs.

CALIFORNIA PORK CHOP BARBECUE

After a long hot drive on a summer weekend, we often used to stop at Love's Barbecue near Los Angeles for a barbecued pork sandwich instead of going home to cook supper. We adored the barbecue, and I was amazed to discover that liquid smoke flavoring was the secret of the heady flavor, though smoke poured from what I thought was the barbecue hut. Commercially prepared smoke flavor is a pure distillate of hickory smoke, but use it with discretion or the concentrated flavor takes on a medicinal taste. I like only a teaspoonful in this sauce.

6 pork chops, 1 inch thick

1½ cups catsup

¼ cup soy sauce

1 to 2 teaspoons liquid smoke

2 tablespoons vinegar

Makes 6 servings.

Grill chops 4 to 6 inches above hot coals, turning to cook evenly, until done but not dry. This will take about 30 minutes.

Meanwhile, in a small saucepan at edge of grill combine catsup, soy sauce, liquid smoke, and vinegar. Stir and heat until well blended. Brush hot sauce on chops and glaze for about 5 minutes over coals. Remove meat to platter and serve with remaining sauce at table.

CAROLINA BARBECUED PORK CHOPS

Meaty center-cut loin chops are sumptuous for this barbecue, but loin end or shoulder chops can be used. Chops cut about an inch thick give you juicy meat.

6 center-cut loin pork chops, 1 inch thick

Carolina Basting Sauce (page 133)

Applesauce or Raisinberry Sauce (page 139)

Makes 6 servings.

Dip chops in basting sauce and place on grill 4 to 6 inches above hot coals. Grill until browned, then turn, baste, and grill on other side until browned. Move to edge of grill and grill until done as desired, turning and basting as necessary to cook evenly and prevent flare-ups. Total cooking time for 1-inch chops will be about 35 minutes. Remove to hot platter and serve with applesauce or Raisinberry Sauce.

GRILLED PORK STEAKS

In my market pork steaks are cut about 1/2 inch thick, so I order ahead and get the butcher to cut me 3/4-inch steaks in order to have the meaty thickness that makes this barbecue juicier and more succulent. Pork steaks are cut from the shoulder.

4 pork steaks, 3/4 inch thick

1/4 cup beef or chicken broth

1/4 cup dry white wine

1 tablespoon minced fresh or 1/2 teaspoon dried rosemary

1 tablespoon minced fresh or 1/2 teaspoon dried
     marjoram

1 clove garlic, smashed

1/2 teaspoon salt

2 tablespoons oil

Makes 4

servings.

Trim as much fat as possible off edges of pork steaks. Place meat in a plastic bag. Combine broth, wine, herbs, garlic, and salt. Add to pork, close bag tightly, and place in dish. Marinate in refrigerator several hours or overnight. Drain pork, reserving marinade.

Grill 4 to 6 inches above medium-hot coals, brushing with marinade now and then and turning to cook evenly. In about 30 minutes, pork should be fully cooked but juicy. Brush with oil and remaining marinade. Serve hot.

SAGE PORK TENDERLOIN

A *clump of sage flourished in an herb bed a few feet from our barbecue grill in Encino, California, so putting a few sprigs of sage on a roast came naturally. If you don't have fresh sage, sprinkle the meat with a couple teaspoons of dried leaf sage.*

1 pork tenderloin, about 2½ pounds

4 to 5 sprigs fresh sage

Salt and freshly ground pepper

Olive oil

Makes 6 to 8 servings.

Slit pork almost through to open out like a book. Place sage in the cavity and sprinkle lightly with salt and pepper. Tie pork into its original shape.

Grill 3 to 4 inches from hot fire until browned, turning to cook evenly. Move to edge of grill and brush with oil. Cover grill or tuck a loose tent of foil around pork to hold in heat. Continue to cook until meat thermometer inserted in center registers 160 degrees, about 35 minutes longer. A few sprigs of fresh sage may be thrown on the fire a few minutes before removing meat from grill. Carve meat in thin slices on board or platter and serve with Sage Butter (see page 143), if desired.

PORK RIBS WITH RAISINBERRY SAUCE

This sauce gives a holiday-like flair to ribs, and you'll think of it for chicken and turkey, too.

4 to 6 pounds spareribs, country-style ribs,
    or back ribs
Rib Seasoning Mix (page 131)
Raisinberry Sauce (page 139)

Makes 4 to 6 servings.

Trim excess surface fat from ribs and sprinkle meat with seasoning mix. Let stand at room temperature about 30 minutes.

Arrange a drip pan at one side or end of grill and push hot coals to back of grill or arrange them around drip pan. Place ribs about 6 inches over hot coals, bone side down, and grill until lightly browned. Turn and brown other side. Move ribs over drip pan, then cover grill or drape a tent of foil loosely over ribs to hold in heat. Cook, turning ribs every 15 minutes, until ribs are done but not charred, about 1 hour. Turn ribs meat side up, drizzle with Raisinberry Sauce, and heat 2 or 3 minutes. Remove ribs to platter; cut into serving-size sections. Serve remaining sauce with ribs.

GINGERED PORK TENDERLOIN

This lean, tender cut of pork is becoming increasingly available due to new cut styles in large pork packing houses. The tenderloin is a favorite of the Chinese and benefits from Oriental-style seasonings, as in this treatment.

1 pork tenderloin, about 2½ pounds

2 cloves garlic, minced

4 thin slices fresh ginger root, or ½ teaspoon
    ground ginger

⅓ cup soy sauce

2 tablespoons sugar

2 tablespoons water

1 tablespoon oil

Makes 12 servings, sliced very thin.

If meat is more than 2½ inches thick, split it into 2 long strips. Place in plastic bag. In a cup combine garlic, ginger, soy sauce, sugar, water, and oil. Pour over meat, close bag tightly, and turn to coat meat well. Place bag in bowl and let meat marinate at room temperature 1 hour or in the refrigerator 3 to 4 hours, turning bag 2 or 3 times. Carefully drain marinade into a small saucepan.

Using a drip pan, cook meat 3 to 4 inches above hot coals, turning to brown evenly, until browned. Move to edge of grill over drip pan; close cover or cover meat loosely with a tent of foil to hold in heat. Grill, turning meat now and then and brushing with marinade about every 5 minutes. Total cooking time will be about 45 minutes. Slice very thin and serve warm with hot mustard or chutney.

Note: This tenderloin can also be served at room temperature or well chilled, so any leftovers are welcome. Thin-sliced pork with a cold noodle salad makes a grand lunch the next day.

CHINESE–STYLE BARBECUED PORK

I was a young woman in Miami when I first had what my date called Chinese roast pork with hot and heavenly sauce. This is my adaptation, after I learned that the restaurateur's "hot and heavenly" is American catsup and mustard.

1/4 cup sweet sherry

1/3 cup soy sauce

1 tablespoon sugar

1 tablespoon grated fresh ginger root

1 clove garlic, minced

1 boneless pork rib end roast, 2 1/2 pounds

1/3 cup catsup

1 tablespoon dry mustard

2 to 3 teaspoons water

Makes 6 to 8 generous servings.

Combine sherry, soy sauce, sugar, ginger, and garlic. Mix well. Place pork in a dish or plastic bag, add sauce, and brush over meat or close bag tightly and turn to coat meat with sauce. Marinate at room temperature 2 to 3 hours or in the refrigerator overnight.

This cut of pork is best cooked on a grill with a cover or on a spit. If you do not have a spit or grill with a cover, shape a loose tent of foil over the meat to hold in heat and help prevent flare-ups while cooking.

Remove meat from marinade, reserving marinade, and place on grill 6 to 8 inches above a drip pan surrounded by hot coals or with coals pushed to the back of the grill. Brush meat with sauce and grill 1 hour, basting and turning as needed to cook evenly and prevent flare-ups. Test with a meat thermometer. When internal temperature reaches 160 degrees, meat is thoroughly cooked but still tender and juicy. A thick roast might require 30 minutes longer.

Just before meat is done, mix catsup into remaining marinade and brush over meat. Turn and glaze meat over drip pan. Remove meat to a platter, cover loosely with foil, and let stand 30 minutes. About 10 minutes before serving, mix dry mustard to a smooth thin paste with water. Thinly slice the pork. Serve catsup sauce and mustard sauce separately, or swirl the mustard into the catsup sauce.

PORK AND APPLES

This is an Indian summer dish, good after the best fall apples come to market.

4 pork loin chops, 1 inch thick, about 2 pounds total

1 cup apple juice

2 tablespoons lemon juice

1 teaspoon leaf sage

2 tablespoons brown sugar

1 onion, minced

2 to 3 firm apples (Greening, Ida Red, Granny Smith)

Salt and freshly ground pepper

Makes 4 servings.

Place meat in a plastic bag. In a small bowl mix apple and lemon juices, sage, brown sugar, and onion and stir until sugar is dissolved. Pour over meat. Close bag tightly and turn to coat chops well with the marinade. Place in a bowl and refrigerate several hours or overnight. Remove chops from marinade and drain well.

Grill about 6 inches above hot coals for 20 minutes, turning and basting with marinade now and then. Core apples but do not peel. Cut in thick rings. Brush apples with marinade and place on grill around pork. Continue grilling pork and apples until pork is done as desired and apples are tender, about 15 minutes. Remove from grill and sprinkle lightly with salt and pepper.

Note: To prepare this combination when good cooking apples are unavailable, open a can of pie-sliced apples (not pie filling) and heat in a skillet with a few bits of pork fat trimmings, a slice or two of onion, and a dash of lemon juice. Serve hot with pork.

DEVILED PORK CUBES

1 to 1¼ pounds boneless pork loin, 1 inch thick

4 thick slices bacon

2 to 3 tablespoons Dijon-style mustard

½ cup fine dry bread crumbs (see Note)

1 tablespoon minced parsley or cilantro (fresh coriander
leaves)

*Makes 4
servings.*

Cut pork into 1-inch cubes. Cut bacon in 1-inch squares. Next, prepare 4 skewers, each of which will hold about 7 cubes of pork and 8 bacon squares. Thread bacon and pork on skewers, starting with bacon, alternating, and ending with bacon. Meat and bacon should not be jammed on but pushed together firmly. Spread a spoonful of mustard on a plate or square of waxed paper and roll each pork skewer in it. Mix bread crumbs with parsley or cilantro on another plate or square of paper. Roll each skewer in this mixture. Skewers can be prepared ahead of time and refrigerated before cooking.

Grill 3 to 4 inches over glowing charcoal, turning to brown evenly. Pork will be juicy and tender but thoroughly cooked in about 20 minutes. Push pork off onto plates with a fork.

Note: I keep fine dry bread crumbs in my freezer. When good French bread dries out, as it often does with the uneven schedule of today's eating, I process it in a blender or with the shredding blade of a food processor. Then I package it in a covered freezer container or bag, and have it ready to go at a moment's notice.

LEMON–GLAZED PORK LOIN

1 boned and tied pork loin, 3½ to 4 pounds
½ cup lemon juice
¼ cup oil
¼ cup soy sauce
2 tablespoons brown sugar
1 tablespoon Dijon-style mustard

Makes 6 servings, with leftovers.

Place drip pan in firebox of grill, pushing hot coals to the back or around drip pan. Place meat over drip pan and grill until browned, turning as needed to cook evenly. Cover grill and adjust dampers so that fire burns slowly. If grill has no cover, place a loose tent of foil over roast to hold in heat.

Meanwhile, mix together lemon juice, oil, soy sauce, brown sugar, and mustard. Beat well to blend. Brush on meat several times while grilling. After 1½ hours test with a meat thermometer. Continue basting and turning meat until internal temperature registers 160 degrees on thermometer. Remove to platter and let stand 20 minutes before carving.

This is good with sweet potatoes roasted on the grill or, in summer, fresh corn on the cob.

SPITTED PORK WITH ORANGE SAUCE

*T*his sauce can be used on lamb, ham, or turkey as well as pork. Orange and smoke flavors are highly regarded by barbecue cooks in Florida. We have used this sauce to barbecue fresh red snapper, too, with fine results.*

1 pork loin or boned and tied loin roast, 4 to 5 pounds
1 cup orange juice
½ cup lemon juice
2 tablespoons soy sauce
1 clove garlic, minced
½ teaspoon ground cloves
⅓ cup sugar
1 tablespoon cornstarch
½ teaspoon cinnamon
1 tablespoon grated orange peel
4 orange slices with peel, halved

Makes 5 to 6 servings.

If using pork with bone, have the butcher crack the backbone for easier carving. Place pork in plastic bag. Mix orange and lemon juices, soy sauce, garlic, and cloves. Pour into bag with pork, close bag tightly, and turn to coat meat with sauce. Place bag in bowl and refrigerate overnight, turning now and then. Remove meat from bag and reserve marinade.

Place meat on spit, making sure it is balanced to turn smoothly, and fasten with spit forks. Engage spit so meat turns about 6 inches above hot coals. Roast meat until meat thermometer registers 160 degrees, about 1½ hours. Remove pork from spit and let stand on board or platter 20 to 30 minutes before carving.

Meanwhile, in a small saucepan mix sugar, cornstarch, cinnamon, and orange peel. Add reserved marinade and cook and stir over medium heat until thickened and translucent, about 5 minutes. Add orange slices to heat through. Serve hot with carved meat.

BARBECUED HAM AND HONEYED PINEAPPLE

This makes a handsome and easy patio supper if you use ham labeled fully cooked, which needs only thorough heating to develop the flavor (see Note).

1 steak cut from a fully cooked whole or semiboneless ham, 2 inches thick

1/2 cup unsweetened pineapple juice

2 tablespoons oil

1 teaspoon prepared mustard, plus 1/4 cup for sauce

1 large ripe pineapple

About 2 tablespoons honey

Makes 6 to 8 servings.

If you are unable to get a thick ham steak, cut your own from a fully cooked ham roll, canned ham, cooked country-cured ham, or a home-baked ham. You will need a meat saw for a ham with bone.

Slash the fat edges of the ham to prevent curling. Place ham in a shallow dish. Beat together pineapple juice, oil, and 1 teaspoon mustard. Pour over ham and marinate at room temperature 1 to 2 hours.

Trim any long lethal spikes off pineapple crown and discard any dried spikes. With a very sharp, heavy knife cut pineapple into 6 or 8 lengthwise wedges. Trim crown for neatness but leave core intact to retain shape of pineapple. Place fruit on a long platter and drizzle with honey. Let stand 1 to 2 hours.

Place ham about 6 inches above hot coals. Brush with marinade. Grill 15 minutes or until browned. Turn and brush with marinade. Arrange pineapple in circle around ham on grill. Turn pineapple often as it tends to burn fast. Cook ham 15 minutes longer and grill pineapple until heated through and tinged with brown. Place ham on warm platter and surround with pineapple. For sauce, mix remaining pineapple marinade with 1/4 cup mustard or thin mustard with pineapple juice to serve as sauce. Slice to serve.

Note: Country ham can be used in this grill supper if you treat it first to prevent its drying out. Have the butcher cut a thick steak from the center (the ends of a whole ham will be ready for boiling and glazing to serve another time). Pour hot water over the thick ham slice and let it stand 2 to 3 hours to moisten the meat and soak out some of the salt. Marinate ham as directed above; then remove from marinade and grill.

KEY WEST ROAST PIG

The holiday aroma of Key West and the Cuban quarter of Miami is that of roasting pig, a tradition of the refugees and cigar workers who live in Key West. This recipe's method is adapted from a fine Key West cook. The first trick is to persuade a butcher that you want an infant pig. Although specialty butchers now cater to the demand for small animals for barbecuing, we have been stuck with pigs as large as 29 pounds. Nonetheless, even the large ones make gustatory events.

1 baby pig, preferably 12 to 18 pounds
4 to 6 sour oranges (much preferred) or limes
About 1 tablespoon dried oregano
3 to 4 cloves garlic, minced
Butter
Watercress, parsley, or other greens, for garnish
Limes, other small citrus (calamondins, tangerines, or
    lemons) or olives, for garnish

Makes 8 to 12 company servings, with leftover pickings.

Order a pig well in advance, begging for a small one so it will rest full-length on the grill. Otherwise, have the pig cut crosswise in half to grill it, then reassemble it for serving. Clear a shelf in the refrigerator.

Have the pig thoroughly cleaned. A few remaining bristles can be pulled out with tweezers or a strawberry huller, or shave bristles with a clean disposable razor. Cut tendons in inside knee joints, front and back, so legs can be folded under pig.

Cut sour oranges (more aromatic than any other citrus) or limes and squeeze generously over and inside pig, rubbing juice into skin and cavity. Rub with oregano and garlic. Leave some of the cut citrus in the cavity. Place the pig in a large bag such as a tall kitchen garbage bag, close with a twist tie, and refrigerate overnight.

About 5½ hours before serving, start fire in grill and let coals burn down. The fire must be replenished periodically while cooking, so a portable grill to supply fresh burning coals should be set up nearby.

Remove pig from bag and skewer or sew the cavity closed, shaping body as roundly as possible. Rub the pig thoroughly with soft butter. Place a lime in the mouth to prop jaws open evenly, as this is the shape that the mouth will take. Skewer legs to the pig in folded position.

Place pig about 10 inches above hot coals, positioning it back side up first. Turn from side to side and back side down, brushing with more butter to keep moist. If ears and snout brown too rapidly, cover with folds of foil to prevent burning, though the crisp ears are delicacies. Add coals as needed to keep fire burning steadily but not flaming.

After 3 to 3½ hours, insert a meat thermometer in an inside joint, being careful not to touch bone. When the thermometer shows an internal temperature of 160 to 165 degrees, pig is done. This may take up to 5 hours total on an uncovered grill or as little as 3 hours on a covered grill. Place pig on a platter; remove strings and skewers and the cooked lime from the mouth. Push a fresh lime in place. Garnish extravagantly with watercress or other greens, placing a ringlet around the neck and, if the pig was cut to fit the grill, a wide sash around the center to cover the cut. Skewer a slice of lime or an olive to each eye.

To carve, cut down the backbone and cut off chops. Cut away legs and carve them into thin slices. The head, ears, and small shank portions usually are picked off the bones or crispy bits of skin gnawed blissfully.

SPIT–BARBECUED HAM

1 piece fully cooked boneless ham, 3 pounds
½ cup honey
½ cup wine vinegar

Makes 8 to 10 servings.

Score the ham with shallow cuts. Place on spit and check to make sure it is balanced. Fasten with spit forks. Push coals to back of firebox and place a drip pan in front. Attach spit so coals are about 4 inches from ham. Engage spit and start motor. Cook ham 40 to 45 minutes, until internal temperature on a meat thermometer reaches 125 degrees.

Beat together honey and vinegar. Brush on ham every 2 or 3 minutes and cook 15 minutes longer. Let sit 10 to 20 minutes before carving.

GINGERY HAM STEAK

4 or 5 thin slices fresh ginger root
1 cup pineapple juice
¼ cup packed brown sugar
1 center-cut ham steak, 1½ to 2 inches thick
1 tablespoon cornstarch
Water

Makes 6 servings.

In a small saucepan combine ginger root, pineapple juice, and brown sugar. Stir over fire at edge of grill until brown sugar is dissolved. Slash fatty edges of ham to prevent curling.

Place ham 4 to 5 inches above hot coals. Grill until lightly browned, about 15 minutes; turn and brown the other side. Brush with sauce and turn and brown first one, then the other side. This will take about 15 minutes.

Just before removing ham from grill, blend cornstarch with a small amount of water to make a thin smooth paste. Stir into remaining basting sauce and cook and stir until smooth and translucent. If too thick, stir in more pineapple juice or water. Slice ham and serve with sauce.

BREAKFAST SAUSAGE KEBABS

Cook a pot of grits (pages 168 and 169) or Country-Fried Potatoes (page 178) at the edge of the grill to go with this weekend breakfast. Toast thick slices of French bread, too.

1 small onion, chopped

2 tablespoons oil

1 small clove garlic, minced

1 (8-ounce) can tomato sauce

2 tablespoons brown sugar

2 pounds pork sausage links

2 apples, quartered

2 green peppers, seeded and cut into chunks

Makes 6 servings.

In a small saucepan cook onion in oil until tender but not browned. Add garlic and cook a minute or 2. Stir in tomato sauce and brown sugar. Keep warm while preparing kebabs. Alternate sausage, apples, and green pepper on skewers, spearing sausages crosswise, slightly diagonally. Prick sausages once or twice each.

Grill 6 inches above hot coals, turning and basting with sauce to cook evenly and prevent burning. Serve sausages, apples, and green pepper hot with any remaining sauce as well as buttered grits or Country-Fried Potatoes and toasted French bread.

SAUSAGE AND PEPPERS

This classic Italian-style knife-and-fork sandwich is peddled from pushcarts at the wildly wonderful Feast of San Gennaro each summer in New York's Little Italy. The pushcarts are equipped with miniature steam tables that keep the sausage and peppers hot. Sausage and peppers grilled over charcoal are even better than on the street, to my taste.

2 medium green bell peppers
2 medium red or yellow bell peppers
1 medium onion
2 large cloves garlic, minced
Salt and freshly ground pepper
2 tablespoons olive oil
1½ pounds sweet or hot Italian sausage
2 long loaves Italian bread, split and toasted

Makes
4 to 6
servings.

Remove seeds and spines from peppers and cut peppers in strips or squares. Pile peppers in center of a large rectangle of heavy-duty aluminum foil (or you can cook this in a skillet with a cover). Peel and slice onion and place over peppers. Sprinkle with garlic, salt, black pepper, and oil. Fold foil over vegetables, allowing space for steam but sealing foil package tightly with a double fold. Place at edge ofgrill in which a hot fire is ready for cooking.

If it is in 1 piece, cut sausage in 3- or 4-inch lengths. Grill sausage over hot coals, browning on all sides while you turn meat and squirt any leaping flames with water to prevent burning. This will take 15 to 18 minutes. When sausages are browned, unwrap or uncover vegetables, protecting hands with a barbecue mitt. Place sausages over pepper mixture and seal packet again. Move to a hotter section of grill and cook until sausages are done through and peppers tender, 10 to 15 minutes longer. Spoon peppers and sausages onto split and toasted bread for mammoth knife-and-fork sandwiches. Cut in large sections.

BARBECUED SAUSAGE

Barbecue guests usually like substantial before-dinner food, and this is perfect — sausage given an extra smoking over your grill and served with sauce. For a light meal, this can be the main dish, with toasted buns and a big bowlful of potato salad.

Smoked, Italian, or big link sausage
Barbecue sauce of your choice (pages 129–41)

Place sausage at edge of grill and heat, turning often. Prick with a fork once or twice to allow excess fat to cook out. When heated through remove to a chopping board, cut in small pieces, spear with picks, and serve with your choice of sauce on the side. If sausage requires cooking, make sure it is thoroughly cooked before serving. Small link sausages can be cooked the same way, but are more difficult to keep track of and require much turning to cook evenly.

POLYNESIAN PORK BURGERS

Old-fashioned ideas of fatty pork no longer hold. Today's pork is so lean that it needs ground beef mixed in to produce a juicy burger.

1½ pounds ground lean pork
½ pound ground lean beef
2 tablespoons soy sauce
½ small green pepper, finely chopped
8 pineapple rings

Makes 8 servings.

Combine pork, beef, soy sauce, and green pepper. Mix lightly but thoroughly. Shape mixture into patties about 1 inch thick.

Grill 4 to 5 inches above hot coals until browned, then turn and brown the other side. Meanwhile, place pineapple rings at edge of grill to warm them. When pork patties are browned, move meat to edge of grill and the pineapple rings to the center. Grill meat and pineapple until done and pineapple begins to brown. Move pineapple rings to tops of pork patties as they brown. Test pork for doneness by cutting into the center of each patty. Juice runs clear or golden, not pink, if pork is done. Serve hot with more soy sauce, if desired.

BEEF

The American ideal of fine eating is a thick steak, grilled juicy and rare inside and charred smoky and full of flavor outside. Americans produce the best beef in the world and many of us appreciate it. A men's club in Santa Maria, California, does a showpiece barbecue with 2½-inch-thick cuts of strip steaks grilled over the local red oak that makes a fire so hot you wonder how the official cooks can stand it. The men have devised an elaborate pulley system to turn the tons of steaks that they grill on occasion for such important events as Republican and Democratic party wingdings. A large number of Presidents during the past thirty years have had Santa Maria barbecued steaks. Perhaps the most unusual out-door cooked steaks that I've had were done in a farmyard near Bismarck, North Dakota. I had been invited to judge the annual National Beef Cook-Off. The evening after the contest awards dinner, the contestants, judges, and other guests were invited to a "pitchfork fondue." A young ranch hand speared two or three thick steaks on a shiny-clean pitchfork and plunged the meat into a huge pot of bubbling hot suet for a few minutes to cook the beef crusty and medium-rare. We had baked potatoes, coleslaw, and good bread with the perfectly cooked meat.

A recipe isn't necessary for pitchfork fondue—only an enormous iron pot, enough suet to fill it about two-thirds full, and the courage to build a fire large enough to heat it. And—oh, yes—a stack of top-quality T-bone or porterhouse steaks and two or three new pitchforks, too.

The recipes in this chapter represent a wide range of cookery styles, from true-blue American steaks and burgers to thin bits of meat flavored Oriental-style.

GRILLED STEAK

A *barbecue enthusiast is likely to be judged on his steaks, no matter how well he does other foods. For best steaks, use a charcoal that burns hot and don't try to hurry the fire. And find a good butcher. Get thick steaks, 1½ to 2 inches thick, because they gain most from charcoal grilling. Club steak can be grilled in a one-person portion, even though this may be too much for small appetites, but the large steaks—sirloins, T-bones, and porterhouse or strip steaks—should be sliced for serving. Steak for grilling should be prime or top of the choice grade and show fine marbling. Coarse marbling usually indicates tough connective tissue.*

If the steak has a thick layer of outer fat, trim it, leaving some fat to keep meat flavorful and tender. Score the fat in several places around the rim of the steak to prevent curling. Remove the steak from the refrigerator at least an hour before grilling it.

Place steaks 2 inches or thicker on grill 5 inches above hot coals; thinner steaks, 3 to 4 inches above coals. Grill until meat juices start to bubble up through top of the steak. Turn, using tongs so as not to pierce and lose juices, and grill until meat juice bubbles up to the second side. Continue grilling and turning until steak is done as desired.

A steak 2 inches thick will be cooked rare in a total of 15 minutes, medium in 20 minutes, and well-done in 25 minutes. Slit the steak near the center with a knife to check for degree of doneness. Steaks 1½ inches thick require about 5 minutes less cooking time, and thicker steaks, up to 2½ inches, require about 20 minutes total grilling for rare, 25 for medium, and 30 for well-done.

To serve, remove steak to a warm platter and slice across the grain; or serve 1 club steak per person.

TEXAS BEEF BARBECUE

This basic Texas barbecue is usually cooked in a Dutch oven or covered roasting pan, with liquid smoke for flavor. I prefer charcoal roasting and a few damp hickory chips on the fire.

1 piece beef brisket, 3½ pounds

1 cup catsup

½ cup cider vinegar

¼ cup Worcestershire sauce

½ stick (¼ cup) butter

3 ribs celery, finely chopped

1 onion, finely chopped

2 cloves garlic, minced

1 fresh or canned green chile, seeded and minced,
    or 2 teaspoons chili powder

1 teaspoon paprika

½ teaspoon salt

½ teaspoon freshly ground pepper

Makes 10 to 12 barbecue sandwiches.

When fire has burned down to hot coals, spread to provide moderate heat and fit a drip pan in front or in center of coals. Place brisket fat side up over drip pan. Cover grill and adjust dampers to maintain slow steady heat.

While meat is cooking, in a saucepan combine all other ingredients and simmer 10 minutes. After 1 hour baste meat lightly with sauce and turn meat as needed to cook evenly. Replenish fire as needed, but don't pile coals, as brisket should cook slowly. Cook 4 to 5 hours total, until meat almost falls apart.

Sprinkle 2 or 3 handfuls of hickory chips that have been soaked in water over coals. Cover grill or enclose top of meat in a sheet of foil tucked around bottom edges of meat and let hickory smoke meat for 10 to 15 minutes. Remove cover and brush meat with sauce. Place meat on platter and slice. It will crumble. Serve meat and remaining sauce on split and buttered sandwich buns.

Any leftover sandwiches can be frozen and reheated in a microwave or conventional oven, or the shredded meat and sauce can be frozen together to reheat later for sandwiches.

HERBED BEEF FILLET

1 beef fillet, about 5 pounds
1 stick (½ cup) butter
1 tablespoon minced fresh or 1 teaspoon dried tarragon
1 tablespoon minced fresh or 1 teaspoon dried chervil
1 tablespoon minced shallots or scallions
2 tablespoons dry white wine
2 tablespoons white wine vinegar

Makes 8 to 10 servings.

Buy a prime fillet, if possible, and fold under and tie tail to form a roast of uniform thickness. Melt butter in a small saucepan. Stir in tarragon, chervil, and shallots or scallions. Cook over very low heat a minute or 2. Slowly stir in wine and vinegar and heat slowly. Place meat on a tray and brush with herbed butter. Let stand at room temperature 1 hour, brushing with sauce 2 or 3 times. Remove meat from tray and pour any sauce remaining on tray into saucepan with remaining sauce.

Brown fillet over coals on all sides for about 10 minutes, watching carefully to prevent fire flare-ups. Move meat to edge of grill or cover grill and adjust dampers to maintain slow steady heat. Grill 15 to 20 minutes longer or until fillet is done as desired. Heat remaining sauce at edge of grill and serve with sliced fillet.

GRILLED FILLET WITH MUSHROOM SAUCE

This lightly hickory-smoked fillet is a favorite of my dear friend Jim Beard. He likes it very rare. The sliced fillet makes good luncheon sandwiches.

1 beef fillet, about 4½ pounds
½ cup red wine
¼ cup oil
¼ cup minced onion
1 tablespoon herbes de Provence or other herb blend
Mushroom Sauce (recipe follows)

Makes 6 to 8 servings.

Buy prime-grade fillet, if possible, and trim it well. Fold and tie the tail to the meat to form a roast of uniform thickness (or have butcher do it for you). Place meat in a plastic bag. Mix wine, oil, onion, and herbs. Pour over the meat, close bag tightly, and turn it to coat meat with marinade. Place bag in a dish and marinate meat 2 hours at room temperature or overnight in refrigerator. Drain meat, reserving marinade.

Grill meat 4 inches above hot coals, turning to brown all sides. This takes about 10 minutes of undivided attention so you can put out any flash fires. Add damp hickory chips or small hickory sticks. Move meat to edge of grill or cover grill and cook 15 to 20 minutes longer for rare, 20 to 25 minutes for medium-rare. Slice and serve with Mushroom Sauce.

MUSHROOM SAUCE

2 tablespoons butter
2 tablespoons minced onion
2 cloves garlic, minced
8 ounces fresh mushrooms, cleaned and sliced
1 teaspoon meat glaze (Bovril) or broth seasoning mix
Reserved marinade for fillet
Red wine or beef broth, if needed

Makes 6 to 8 servings.

In a medium skillet melt butter, add onion and garlic, and cook until onion is tender but not browned. Add mushrooms and cook, stirring gently now and then, until well saturated with butter and most of the juices cooked from mushrooms have evaporated. Stir in meat glaze. Add reserved marinade and, if needed, a few tablespoons wine or broth to make a light sauce. Serve hot with grilled fillet.

BEEF–FILLED ONIONS

3 large onions
1½ pounds lean ground beef
1 egg, slightly beaten
1 teaspoon salt
Florida or Texas barbecue sauce (page 135 or 136)

*Makes 6
servings.*

Cut onions in half crosswise, pull off skins, and scoop out centers, leaving sturdy shells. Chop scooped-out onion. Combine beef, egg, salt, ¾ cup sauce, and the chopped onion. Mix well and shape into 6 large meatballs. Cut 6 squares of heavy-duty foil large enough to contain each onion half, and place an onion half on each of the squares. Put a meatball in each onion half and spoon a little sauce over the combination. Fold foil up around onions and seal tightly, allowing space in foil packets for steam.

Grill 4 to 6 inches above hot coals about 30 minutes. Protecting hands with mitts, peel back foil so tops of meat and onions are exposed. Baste with drippings in foil packets or with additional sauce. Cover grill or shape a loose tent of foil over onions and continue cooking 25 minutes longer or until onions are as tender as desired and meat is done to taste.

BARBECUED BEEF RIBS

"Ribs for barbecue" were abundant in markets for a few years, now I find them only occasionally. Though they are scarce, it is worth knowing this special cut. The ribs grill crusty and have a big bone to gnaw on after you've cut off the dainty slivers of meat. Make sure you get rib bones; short ribs are too tough to barbecue.

    2 or 3 rib bones per person
    Barbecue sauce of your choice (pages 129–41) or
        Dijon-style mustard

Place ribs rounded side down on grill 3 to 4 inches above hot coals. Brown, turn, and brown the other side. Brush lightly with barbecue sauce or mustard. Cook and turn until done as desired, about 10 minutes for ribs with an average amount of sauce. Heat sauce at edge of grill and serve at table with ribs, or pass extra mustard.

GRILLED SKIRT STEAK

This flat fibrous steak is richly flavored when grilled over charcoal, and the marinade enhances the effect. Don't overcook a skirt steak or it will be dry and tough.

    1 teaspoon dry mustard
    1 teaspoon ground cumin
    1 bay leaf, crumbled
    1 clove garlic, minced
    1 cup well-seasoned beef broth, heated to boiling
    1/4 cup Worcestershire sauce
    1 tablespoon cider vinegar
    1 tablespoon oil
    1 teaspoon hot pepper sauce
    2 skirt steaks, about 12 ounces each

Makes 4 servings.

In a small bowl or 2-cup measure blend mustard, cumin, bay leaf, and garlic. Add boiling broth and mix well, mashing any lumps of mustard against side of bowl or cup. Stir in Worcestershire sauce, vinegar, oil, and pepper sauce. Cover and let cool.

Place steaks in a plastic bag or shallow dish, add marinade, turn, and let marinate 2 to 3 hours at room temperature, turning 2 or 3 times. Remove meat from marinade and grill 4 to 5 inches above hot coals until well browned, 6 to 8 minutes; turn and brown other side for 6 to 8 minutes. Brush with marinade and serve at once.

Any leftover marinade can be frozen and reused.

LEMON–GARLIC FLANK STEAK

Many regard this as the tastiest of all steaks. But be sure to carve it imme-diately after it comes off the grill—otherwise, the fibers tighten and the steak becomes leathery. Have a sharp knife and board ready to slice it thin across the grain. Any extras should be sliced immediately and kept in the refrigerator for tomorrow's lunch.

1 flank steak, about 1½ pounds
½ medium sweet onion, thinly sliced and separated
    into rings
⅓ cup lemon juice
1 clove garlic, split
1 tablespoon sugar
½ teaspoon salt
2 tablespoons soy sauce

Makes 4 to 6 servings.

Pull off any membrane from steak and trim away any surface fat. Score steak ⅛ inch deep on both sides in diamond pattern. In plastic bag or glass dish large enough to hold steak, combine onion, lemon juice, garlic, sugar, salt, and soy sauce. Add steak, close bag tightly if using, and turn meat to coat thoroughly. Marinate 1 to 2 hours at room temperature, 6 to 8 hours in the refrigerator. Drain off and reserve marinade.

Grill steak 3 to 5 inches above hot coals until rare to medium-rare, 3 to 5 minutes on each side. Meanwhile, heat remaining marinade. Remove steak to a cutting board and cut in thin slices across the grain, slanting knife slightly. Serve meat with hot marinade.

GRILLED CALF'S LIVER STEAK

My friend Jerome Schilling, an architect, literally designed his home in Miami Shores, Florida, around the barbecue grill. You open the front door and are greeted with a dramatic vista of a tropical garden, then move through the living room, past his wife Louise's artfully set table, to the kitchen. The kitchen opens onto the grill, built to the leeward side to prevent cooking fumes from wafting indoors. There Jerome cooks. He has introduced me to dozens of the delights of barbecuing, and I particularly enjoy feasting on this thick liver steak when I visit the Schillings.

2 pounds calf's liver, cut 1 to 1½ inches thick

1 large onion, cut in 4 slices

1 stick (½ cup) butter, melted

Salt and freshly ground pepper

Juice of ½ lemon

4 slices bacon, cooked crisp

Makes 4 generous servings.

Dip liver and onion slices in melted butter and place on grill 4 to 6 inches above hot fire. Grill until liver and onion are browned; turn and grill the other sides. Place onion on top of liver and grill until meat is done as desired. The liver is best if crusty on the outside and still pink inside. Cut a slit in the center of each piece of liver to test for doneness.

Remove liver to a small platter and cut in thin slices. Season with salt, pepper, and lemon juice. Arrange onion slices and bacon on platter around liver.

BEEF

ROAST BEEF IN BOURBON SAUCE

This beef is roasted on a spit, or you can do it on a flat grill if you keep the fire moderate and use a drip pan.

½ cup oil

½ cup bourbon

1 onion, thinly sliced

2 cloves garlic, minced

1 teaspoon freshly ground pepper

1 teaspoon dry mustard

1 teaspoon salt

¼ cup wine or cider vinegar

1 rib-eye or tied prime or choice grade first-cut chuck
    or boneless beef round, 5 to 6 pounds

Makes 10 to 12 generous servings.

Combine oil, bourbon, onion, garlic, pepper, mustard, salt, and vinegar. Place meat in plastic bag or dish. Pour marinade over meat and marinate 1 hour at room temperature, turning meat 2 or 3 times.

Drain meat, reserving marinade. Spit meat from end to end through center or on a diagonal, making sure roast is balanced. If the meat has not already been tied, tie it after you have fastened it in place with spit forks — it will be a little firmer that way.

Engage spit and turn meat 8 to 10 inches above hot coals 1½ hours (or until meat thermometer registers 120 degrees) for rare, to 2½ hours for well-done (165 degrees internal temperature). Brush with sauce last 30 minutes of cooking. To roast on grill, place meat over drip pan with hot coals surrounding it or pushed to back, and turn and baste meat as needed to cook evenly. Grill 1½ to 2½ hours. Let meat stand on platter 20 to 30 minutes before carving. Heat sauce and serve with meat.

Leftovers make grand sandwiches and beef salad.

PEPPERED ROUND STEAK

⅓ cup olive oil

1½ to 2 pounds top round steak, 1½ inches thick

2 tablespoons balsamic or red wine vinegar

Freshly ground pepper

Makes 4 generous servings.

Heat oil until very warm, not sizzling. Place meat in a shallow dish and pierce all over with a fork. Turn and pierce other side. Pour half the warm oil on meat and poke with fork so oil penetrates meat fibers. Turn and repeat process on the other side. Pour vinegar over steak and turn. Cover and marinate at room temperature about 2 hours or in refrigerator overnight, turning and piercing meat occasionally. Remove meat, reserving marinade, and sprinkle pepper over generously, pressing it in with the heel of the hand.

Grill meat 3 inches above hot coals until browned; turn and grill other side. Move to edge of grill and continue cooking until done as desired. This steak is most tender if grilled rare, about 18 minutes' total cooking time, or medium-rare, about 22 minutes. Place on warm platter and slice across the grain. Serve with Shallot Cream (recipe follows), if desired.

SHALLOT CREAM

2 tablespoons marinade for Peppered Round Steak

1 tablespoon minced shallots

1 cup heavy cream

Salt and coarsely ground pepper

In a small skillet heat marinade. Stir in shallots and cook until lightly browned. Stir in cream and cook, stirring often, until slightly reduced. Season to taste with salt and pepper. Serve with steak.

BISTECES RANCHEROS

Near my New York apartment, a pretty little restaurant with a few Taos-style paintings hanging on the pink walls serves this spicy supper dish. If you can get good tortillas, this is a snap to make—a good beefy flavor with Tex-Mex verve.

2 pounds chuck steak

1 clove garlic, smashed

1/3 cup olive oil

12 corn tortillas

2 or 3 canned long green chiles, cut in 12 strips

Santa Maria Salsa (page 185)

Makes 6 servings.

Cut steak into fingers 1 by 1 by 3 inches. In a plastic bag combine steak with garlic and oil. Close tightly and turn to coat meat well. Marinate at room temperature for 1 to 1½ hours.

Grill steak 3 to 4 inches from hot coals, turning to brown evenly. Meat should be rare to medium-rare. This takes 10 to 12 minutes' total cooking time.

Meanwhile, wrap tortillas in a clean kitchen towel and heat in a 325-degree oven. As meat comes off fire, place a strip of steak and a strip of chile in each tortilla and roll up. Serve with Santa Maria Salsa. Two of these fat tortilla sandwiches make a nice portion, served with refried beans or beans and rice.

BEEF SATAY

The first time I ate grilled skewered beef strongly seasoned with lime juice, honey, soy sauce, and spices was in a restaurant operated by an Indonesian man in Santa Monica, California. Since then I've had similar skewered beef or pork in the Thai restaurants that are springing up all over the country, as well as in Indian, Malaysian, and Vietnamese restaurants.

2 pounds beef sirloin or fillet

½ cup soy sauce

2 tablespoons honey

2 tablespoons lime juice

1 tablespoon curry powder

1 teaspoon chili powder

1 medium onion, minced

2 cloves garlic, minced

Makes 6 main-dish servings; 12 to 15 appetizer servings.

Cut meat in 1-inch cubes and place in a bowl or plastic bag. In a 2-cup measure combine soy sauce, honey, lime juice, curry and chili powders, onion, and garlic. Mix thoroughly and pour over meat. Marinate 30 minutes at room temperature. Thread meat on bamboo skewers that have been soaked in water to prevent charring or on small metal skewers. Push meat close together if some rare portions are wanted, space it slightly for well-done meat.

Grill 2 to 3 inches above hot coals until done as desired, about 8 minutes total for medium-rare.

KIELBASA GRILL ALFRESCO

A *fast-cooking skewerful of spicy sausage, apple, and onion is a good thought for a campfire breakfast, or a nourishing supper when you are too tired or rushed to fuss.*

1 pound kielbasa or Polish sausage

2 or 3 firm, tart apples (McIntosh, Ida Red, Jonathan, or Granny Smith)

2 or 3 onions

Makes 4 to 6 servings.

Cut kielbasa in 1½-inch slices. Wash and cut unpeeled apples in 4 to 6 wedges each. Peel onions and cut in half, then in wedges. You will need 8 to 12 wedges. Thread sausage chunks with apple and onion wedges on skewers, alternating meat with apple and onion and starting and ending with sausage. Apples and onions should be speared diagonally so they don't slip off while cooking.

Grill 3 inches above hot coals until browned and done as desired, about 12 minutes' total cooking for juicy but well-cooked sausage. Push meat and accompaniments off skewers onto warm plates, using a fork. Serve with mustard along with baked potatoes or poppyseed noodles.

BEEF TERIYAKI

Tangy sweet teriyaki sauce perks up steaks or hamburgers, but accordion-threaded skewers of thin-cut beef make the traditional Japanese teriyaki.

1 top round or chuck steak, at least 1 inch thick,
  2 to 3 pounds
½ cup catsup
¼ cup teriyaki sauce
¼ cup water
2 tablespoons honey
1 clove garlic, minced

Makes 4 to 6 main-dish servings.

Partially freeze meat, then with very sharp knife cut into almost paper-thin strips across the grain. There should be 3 to 4 strips of meat for each person. Fold meat accordion-style onto bamboo skewers that have been soaked in water to prevent charring or short metal skewers. Place in a shallow bowl or plastic bag. Combine catsup, teriyaki sauce, water, honey, and garlic. Mix well and pour over meat on skewers. Turn and marinate in sauce about 30 minutes.

Grill 2 to 3 inches over hot fire on hibachi or small grill until browned, but not dried out, about 4 minutes' total cooking time. Serve as hors d'oeuvres or as a main dish with rice and Japanese-style vegetables.

KOREAN BEEF BARBECUE

This fast barbecue holds to the Oriental system of thin-cut meat to conserve precious fuel. Use a hibachi or small grill, since a big fire will still be burning long after the meat is cooked.

1½ pounds boneless beef chuck, round, or sirloin,
    cut 1 inch thick

1 tablespoon sesame seeds

1 cup finely chopped scallions (2 large)

2 to 3 cloves garlic, minced

¼ cup soy sauce

2 tablespoons sugar

2 tablespoons dry sherry

2 tablespoons vegetable oil

Makes
4 to 6
servings.

Freeze meat until firm, about 2 hours. Meanwhile, in a heavy skillet spread sesame seeds and toast over moderate heat until golden. Stir seeds once or twice to toast evenly. With mortar and pestle or with back of a spoon against a board, grind seeds until powdery. Place in a large bowl with scallions, garlic, soy sauce, sugar, sherry, and oil. Mix well.

With a very sharp knife, cut semifrozen meat across the grain into strips about ¼ inch thick. Add meat strips to sauce, stir to coat meat well, cover, and marinate at room temperature 1 to 2 hours.

Let fire in hibachi or small grill burn down to glowing coals. If grill rack is widely spaced, place meat strips in a hinged wire broiler. Broil about 1 minute on each side until browned but still rare. Serve with rice and vinegary coleslaw or cucumber salad.

STUFFED HAMBURGERS PLUS

Plump burgers grilled over wood or charcoal fire are plenty good, but a filling makes them a Saturday night special for guests. The fillings can also be used as toppings, if you prefer.

2 pounds lean ground beef (see Note)
4 to 6 ounces sharp Cheddar cheese
Barbecue sauce of your choice (pages 129–41)

Makes 6 thick stuffed patties.

Shape the meat into 12 thin patties, pressing just enough to make meat cling together. Cut cheese in slivers and arrange on half the patties, leaving space to seal edges. Place remaining patties over cheese and press edges firmly to seal.

Grill 4 to 5 inches above hot coals until browned on both sides, turning as needed to cook evenly. Cook until done as desired, about 10 minutes' total cooking for rare, 12 to 15 minutes for medium, and 15 to 18 minutes for well-done. Serve hot on toasted buns with catsup, mustard, pickle relish, or other condiments.

Note: Beef labeled lean or ground chuck, not very lean or leanest, makes juicy burgers without excessive shrinking.

OTHER FILLINGS:

Cheese spread: pepper-flavored, herb-flavored, or chive cheese — a good way to use up leftover party cheeses.

Butter blended half and half with crumbled Roquefort or other blue cheese; a flavored butter (see pages 142–4); 6 tablespoons soft butter blended with 1 to 2 tablespoons Dijon-style mustard or prepared horseradish.

Mushrooms and shallots sautéed in butter; thinly sliced tomato or green pepper rings; sliced onion.

HOLLYWOOD BURGERS

Back in the sixties, one of the first stylish "health food" restaurants in Hollywood, the Aware Inn, served plump juicy hamburgers like these.

1½ pounds ground lean beef
1½ cups shredded Cheddar cheese
½ cup each chopped seeded fresh tomato, seeded green
    pepper, and onion
½ teaspoon sea salt or kosher salt
Freshly ground pepper to taste

Makes 4 large or 6 medium-size servings.

Combine beef, cheese, tomato, green pepper, onion, salt, and pepper to taste. Work together with hands until well mixed. Shape into patties, pressing gently to make meat and vegetables cling together.

Grease grill well. Place patties on grill 3 to 4 inches above hot coals and grill until well browned, turning to cook evenly. Cook until done as desired, rare in about 12 minutes, medium in about 15, and well-done in 18 to 20 minutes.

HAMBURGERS WITH CHILI

2 cups chili con carne, leftover homemade or canned
1½ cups shredded Cheddar cheese
½ cup California red table wine
1½ pounds lean ground beef
½ teaspoon salt
2 tablespoons grated onion
4 slices toasted French bread

Makes 4 generous servings.

In a small saucepan combine chili, cheese, and wine. Heat at edge of grill, stirring now and then, until cheese is melted and blended into chili. Meanwhile, mix beef, salt, and onion. Shape into 4 patties about 1 inch thick.

Grill 3 to 4 inches above hot coals until done as desired, 10 to 12 minutes for medium-rare. Place on toast and spoon cheese chili over them.

AL VELA'S BARBECUED BEEF

The excuse for driving the horrendous road from Los Angeles to San Quintin Bay in Baja California — it was in the sixties and some of the road was unpaved, dusty, and full of ruts — was to fish. But the reason Jim and Ann Hanyen, my husband, and I chose Al Vela's El Molino Viejo over other more accessible places was his table. Al always cooked, with the help of local women and his wife, Dorothy. Having grown up in Sonora, Al worked in Santa Monica, California, for a few years, then took his young family to San Quintin to operate a sardine cannery. In the fifties, when sardine fisheries lagged, he converted the canning plant to a hunting and fishing lodge. His meals became legendary, drawing many a traveler from North America. Almost every evening at dinner, we overnighters were joined by a sophisticated group of seed salesmen, campers, and tourists en route to Cabo San Lucas.

I remember the night Al served barbecued local beef, always of dubious quality, with the coarse corn that Mexicans insist on growing, fresh snap beans, and a pie that Dorothy had made of canned condensed milk and limes, just plucked from the tree. The food at El Molino was particularly remarkable because Al had to depend heavily on pantry items — it was 100 miles to Ensenada and the nearest grocery store.

I can also recall the reaction of a young Frenchwoman, a reluctant guest whose husband had lost his way on the dreadful road, when she tasted Al's beef, fresh corn dressed simply with cream, finely chopped onion, and fresh cilantro. Her eyes lit up and she said, "You've done something special to this food!" Al always stands near to hear comments and insure good service by the waitresses. At the Frenchwoman's comment, he brought out bottles of Cabernet Sauvignon, Baja-made by a gifted winegrower.

I had found Al barbecuing the beef the afternoon before. I recognized it as Mexican-cut beef, in nondescript hunks. Al swore me to secrecy. The beef had been slaughtered a few miles away that morning. Al sped back to the lodge with it and refrigerated the meat to take the body heat out of it. I found him searing it rapidly over a charcoal fire, then braising it gently in a skillet of barbecue sauce. "You have to nurse this beef along," Al explained.

If you get beef that is not up to your expectations, or have a less tender cut, try Al's method.

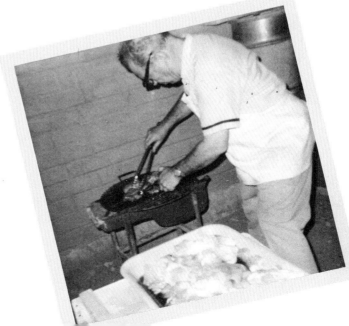

2 pounds beef round, chuck, or shank, cut in serving-
    size pieces
Barbecue sauce of your choice (pages 129–41)

Makes
6 to 8
servings.

Brown meat quickly on grill 3 to 4 inches above very hot coals to seal in juices. At edge of grill heat about 1/2 inch of barbecue sauce in a large skillet with a cover. As each small steak is browned, place it in the sauce. After all the meat is seared and piled in the skillet, brush lightly with additional sauce, cover the skillet, and braise meat 10 minutes, just until moist and heated through, but not well-done. If overcooked, the meat will be dry and stringy. Spread hot coals out to lower heat. With tongs, lift steaks onto grill over moderate heat and cook just long enough to crisp the surface. Serve at once with any leftover sauce, if desired.

LONDON BROIL

Flank steak is the traditional cut for London broil, though a thick top round is labeled London Broil in some markets. The marinade works on either cut.

1 flank steak or top round, 1½ to 2 pounds
1 large clove garlic, split
2 tablespoons oil
1 tablespoon red wine vinegar
Salt and freshly ground pepper
1 stick (½ cup) butter
¼ cup beef broth
¼ cup dry red wine
1 teaspoon Worcestershire sauce
2 tablespoons minced fresh parsley
1 tablespoon minced scallion tops

Makes 4 to 6 servings.

Cut meat on each side into 1½-inch diamonds about ⅛ inch deep. Rub with garlic and place in a shallow dish. Sprinkle with oil, vinegar, and salt and pepper to taste. Turn in dish, cover, and marinate at room temperature 30 to 45 minutes.

Meanwhile, melt butter and stir in broth, wine, Worcestershire sauce, parsley, and scallions. Keep warm on edge of grill.

Grill steak 3 to 4 inches above hot coals 4 to 5 minutes on each side for flank, 6 to 8 minutes for round. Do not overcook, or flank steak will be tough. Immediately remove to board and, holding knife almost parallel with meat, carve in very thin diagonal slices. Serve with the wine and herb sauce.

CHUCK STEAK WITH DEVILED SAUCE

1 chuck steak, 2½ pounds, about 1½ inches thick
Olive oil
¼ cup finely chopped scallions
½ cup soy sauce
¼ cup catsup
1 tablespoon prepared mustard
1 teaspoon freshly ground pepper

Makes 4 to 6 servings.

Place steak in dish and puncture with fork in several places, then drizzle with olive oil. In a small saucepan combine 2 tablespoons olive oil, the scallions, soy sauce, catsup, mustard, and pepper. Heat until well blended and just boiling.

Meanwhile, grill steak 2 to 3 inches above hot coals until browned on both sides, about 30 minutes for medium-rare. Place steak on platter and carve across the grain in ¼-inch slices. Serve 2 or 3 slices per person, with sauce on the side.

GRILLED VEAL CHOPS

Lightly seasoned veal chops grilled quickly over charcoal or a wood fire in a fireplace are juicy and full of flavor.

4 veal loin or shoulder chops, about ¾ inch thick
Salt and freshly ground pepper
Marjoram or thyme
Olive oil
Wine vinegar or lemon juice

Makes 4 servings.

Place veal on a platter and sprinkle lightly with seasonings of choice. Drizzle oil over veal, using about ½ teaspoonful for each side of each chop. Sprinkle with vinegar or lemon juice.

Place 3 to 4 inches over hot fire and grill until browned. Turn and brown other side. Total cooking time will be about 8 minutes. Do not overcook or veal will be tough.

Serve with sautéed mushrooms and boiled potatoes or Country-Fried Potatoes (see page 178).

LAMB

A sheep grower of Greek ancestry and his handsome family once did the most spectacular lamb barbecue I've ever seen. They barbecued eleven lambs in a plaza at the center of Vail, Colorado, to celebrate a bicycle race through the winding streets of the resort town, and I was invited by the lamb growers to participate. The lambs had been slaughtered and dressed the day before, then marinated overnight in a light sauce of lemon and herbs. The whole lambs were put on enormous spits (large enough to serve as small sailboat masts), two lambs to each spit except for the odd one that was on a spit alone. Two of the sheepman's dark-eyed sons hand-turned the spits every 15 minutes or so, when the meat on one side was sizzling and browned, and they turned and basted the lamb from dawn until about 1 p.m., when the feast was served. The wood fires were laid in strips, like bean hills, just to the leeward side of the lambs so that the fat dripped in trenches dug for the purpose. Bicycle racers were *given* tickets to the barbecue, while several hundred vacationers and townspeople bought tickets to share the food—freshly carved lamb piled high on trays, salads, pilaf, and good Greek bread. The sheepman's wife and daughters provided baklava, and the same daughter who had herded several hundred sheep down a mountain the day before poured iced tea.

Lamb is ideal for barbecue because of its natural tenderness and delicate flavor. Wood or charcoal smoke gives lamb special zest. I've barbecued lamb with my family in Florida, in California, and even on my apartment terrace in New York.

The mutton barbecues of western Kentucky are legendary. Alben Barkley, U.S. Senator and later Vice-President, once joked that a Kentucky politician's skill at getting votes was in direct proportion to his level of eloquence after a healthy serving of barbecued mutton. Churches and men's clubs would put on the barbecues as fund-raisers, with one or two amateur chefs in charge of the cooking at each spot, and politicians would invariably come to speak to the crowds gathered for some traditional Kentucky food.

The mutton for the Kentucky barbecues is grown and slaughtered locally. If you find robust-flavored mutton in a market buy some, as the tender cuts are superb for grilling rare and juicy. The recipes here, however, are worked out for young lamb, easily available from good butchers and supermarkets almost everywhere.

BASQUE LAMB BARBECUE

The Kern County Sheepmen's Picnic in Bakersfield, California, is a joyful reunion of two or three thousand sheepmen, their families, and friends. Basque sheepherders who came to this country before the 1960s often stayed to become permanent settlers, buying a few sheep to start and gradually building their herds, and some going into other businesses. The picnic is held in late summer, usually on a blistering hot day, but it is always a gala event, with a sheep auction, dance troupes in costume that come from as far away as San Francisco, men squirting red wine from their sheepskin botas, women showing off children, and everybody eating the barbecued lamb steaks, potato salad, salsa, and chili beans. I marvel at the efficiency of the volunteer chefs who barbecue the lamb, marinating it overnight in barrels of this sauce. I have adapted their way to home-size barbecuing.

½ cup oil

½ cup wine vinegar

½ cup dry white wine

1 clove garlic, minced

½ teaspoon rubbed sage

1 teaspoon salt

¼ teaspoon freshly ground pepper

6 lamb steaks cut from the leg or shoulder, ¾ inch thick

Makes 6 servings.

In a shallow dish combine oil, vinegar, wine, garlic, sage, salt, and pepper. Add lamb and turn to coat well. Cover and marinate at room temperature 2 hours or 24 to 36 hours in the refrigerator, turning once or twice. Bring to room temperature in marinade before grilling.

Drain lamb and grill 4 inches above hot coals 8 to 10 minutes on each side or until done as desired. Lamb fat and the marinade will make the fire flare up, so have a water pistol or bottle of water nearby to extinguish flames. Basque picnic chefs serve lamb steaks with Santa Maria Salsa (see page 185), California Chili Beans (see page 156), My Grandmother's Potato Salad (see page 180), and good bread.

VINEYARD BUTTERFLIED LEG OF LAMB

We once drove up the Napa Valley on a summer afternoon when the grapes were filling out to hang heavy on the vines. Stopping to buy a few bottles of wine, we noticed the heavy aroma of barbecuing lamb in the air. I followed my nose and found the winegrower's wife basting lamb with a sauce made of Zinfandel rosé, garlic, and curry powder. Rosés made of Zinfandel have more character than some sweeter pink luncheon wines called rosés. In fact Zinfandel rosé and the other light Zinfandels are excellent wines to drink with barbecue.

1 butterflied leg of lamb, 4 to 5 pounds
2 cloves garlic, minced
2 teaspoons curry powder
1 cup Zinfandel rosé or other California pink or light
    red wine
Salt and freshly ground pepper
3 tablespoons currant or apple jelly

Makes 6 to 8 servings, with leftovers.

Place lamb in a shallow dish or plastic bag. In a small bowl, mix together the garlic, curry powder, wine, salt and pepper to taste, and the jelly. Beat until well blended. Pour marinade over lamb, turn, and marinate 1 to 2 hours at room temperature.

Place lamb on grill 4 to 6 inches above hot fire, reserving marinade. Brown lamb, brush lightly with marinade, turn, and brown the other side. Cover grill or fit a loose tent of foil over lamb to hold in heat. Turn and brush meat with marinade as needed to cook evenly and prevent flare-ups. Allow 30 to 40 minutes for rare to medium-rare lamb or 50 to 60 minutes for more well-done meat. Slice to serve.

GRILLED BUTTERFLIED
LEG OF LAMB

A *butterflied leg of lamb has thick and thin spots, so there are slices for guests who like well-done lamb and other portions for those who prefer juicy rare meat. I've had butchers in New York, California, Florida, and Alabama who boned and flattened the leg of lamb for me, but if your butcher won't butterfly a lamb leg for you, doing it yourself is not difficult.*

1 leg of lamb, 5 to 6 pounds

2 tablespoons olive oil

1/4 cup wine vinegar

1 to 2 cloves garlic, minced

6 or 8 leafy sprigs fresh mint, or 1 teaspoon dried
    mint flakes

Makes 6 to 8 servings, with leftovers.

Have butcher butterfly leg of lamb. Save the bones, as they make a rich base for barley and mushroom soup or other soups. If you must cut the lamb yourself, use a sharp butcher knife and a slender-bladed boning knife. Cut the meat to the bone, starting at the shank end and slitting toward the butt end. Pull meat away from bone, cutting as needed to loosen it smoothly. Work boning knife around knobby bones. When detached from bones, cut lamb almost through horizontally, then flatten by pressing with the heel of your hand.

In a small saucepan combine oil, vinegar, and garlic. Add mint flakes, if fresh mint is not available. Heat until sizzling.

Baste lamb with sauce and grill 4 to 5 inches above hot coals, turning and basting as needed to cook evenly and prevent flare-ups. Grill 30 to 40 minutes for rare to medium-rare lamb; up to 1 hour for more well-done portions.

If fresh mint is available, line a warm platter with leafy sprigs. Place lamb on mint, which will emit a minty aroma and scent the lamb faintly. Carve lamb in slices on board and arrange on platter to serve with pilaf or baked potatoes and a big salad. Any leftovers make hearty sandwiches on split sourdough or French bread rolls the next day.

LAMB CHOPS WITH PEPPERS

Red peppers are used increasingly since they're imported year-round now from Holland, where they grow in hothouses, but my friend Marlene Guerry says they've been a mark of good Basque cookery for generations.

4 sweet red peppers

4 lamb chops or steaks, 1 inch thick

1/2 teaspoon garlic salt

1 teaspoon Worcestershire sauce

1 teaspoon vinegar

1 tablespoon oil

1 clove garlic, minced

2 or 3 tablespoons olive oil

Makes 4 servings.

Peppers can be prepared ahead of time and refrigerated, or frozen with a little salt and oil sprinkled over them. Spear each pepper on a fork and hold over a hot grill fire or gas flame, or place peppers in a greased shallow baking dish and bake in a very hot oven (450 degrees), until skins wrinkle. Place peppers in cold water and peel off skins. Cut out stems and remove seeds and ribs, keeping peppers whole, if possible. Have peppers at room temperature before cooking.

Rub lamb chops on both sides with garlic salt, Worcestershire sauce, vinegar, and oil. Let stand at room temperature 30 minutes.

Grill lamb 4 inches above hot coals. In a skillet at edge of grill heat minced garlic in olive oil. Add prepared peppers and sauté slowly while cooking lamb. Grill and turn lamb until done as desired, about 8 minutes on each side for rare to 12 minutes on each side for well-done. Place a pepper on each lamb chop and remove to platter.

ROSEMARY LAMB CHOPS

Rosemary is planted on hillsides in Southern California to discourage
flower-eating deer from invading gardens. This herb grows easily in almost any
sunny spot, with little or no care, so try a plant in your garden. I've even grown
it on a windowsill in New York City. To be able to pluck a handful of sprigs to
season lamb chops is a bonus to having the pretty little plant around.

6 rib or loin lamb chops, 1½ inches thick
6 large sprigs fresh or dried rosemary
Olive oil
Salt and freshly ground pepper

Makes 6 servings.

Place chops 3 to 4 inches above hot coals and place a sprig of rosemary
on each or sprinkle chops with rosemary. Brush with oil and grill until
browned. Turn, moving the sprig of rosemary to rest on the grill underneath each chop, and brown other side of chops. (Dried rosemary will cling
when chops are turned.) Cook and turn, basting with oil as needed, until
lamb is done as desired, 15 to 18 minutes for medium-rare to 25 minutes for
well-done.

MINT LAMB CHOPS

8 loin or rib lamb chops, 1½ inches thick,
    about 3 pounds
1 tablespoon dried mint flakes or minced fresh
    mint leaves
2 tablespoons wine vinegar
Salt and freshly ground pepper to taste

Makes 4 large or 8 medium- size servings.

Trim excess fat from edges of chops. Place chops in a shallow dish and
sprinkle with mint and vinegar. Marinate at room temperature 30 minutes
to 1 hour. Remove chops from marinade, shaking off as much as possible.

Grill 4 inches above hot coals until browned, brush with vinegar
mixture, turn, and grill other side until browned. Move to edge of grill and
cook until medium-rare. For 1½-inch chops this requires 15 to 18 minutes'
total cooking time. Remove to warm platter and sprinkle with salt and
pepper. Garnish with fresh mint or watercress.

MIXED GRILL KEBABS

In Turkish and East Indian cookery, shish kebab means meat grilled on skewers, usually with vegetables. The meat is heavily spiced and when you walk along the streets in cities of the Middle East you can smell an exotic blend of spices from street grills or wafting from people's kitchens.

This gourmand's version of shish kebab was invented by my husband Luther by adding one idea to another until he had the most mixed-up skewerful of meat I've ever seen. It was a favorite summertime party dish, since the only accompaniment you needed was bread to sop up the meat and vegetable juices.

1½ pounds leg of lamb, cut in 1½-inch cubes

1 pound boneless tender sirloin of beef,
    cut in 1½-inch cubes

¼ cup oil

½ cup dry red wine

2 tablespoons wine vinegar

½ teaspoon thyme

2 tablespoons minced scallions or shallots

12 to 18 mushroom caps

12 small whole onions, about 1 pound

¾ pound calf's liver, cut in 1-inch cubes

About ½ pound bacon

2 green peppers, seeded and cut in 1-inch squares

Salt and freshly ground pepper

Makes 6 servings.

In a large bowl combine lamb, beef, oil, wine, vinegar, thyme, and scallions or shallots. Mix well. Cover and marinate in refrigerator 4 hours or longer, stirring several times with a spoon. Simmer mushrooms about 2 minutes in boiling water to prevent splitting when threading on skewers. Cut off ends of onions and simmer onions in water 5 minutes or until skins slip off easily; then slip off skins. Wrap cubes of liver in a half strip of bacon each.

Drain lamb and beef, reserving marinade. Alternate lamb, beef, and bacon-wrapped liver with vegetables on 6 skewers. Refrigerate until ready to cook.

Grill 3 to 4 inches above hot coals 25 to 30 minutes, basting with reserved marinade as needed and turning to cook evenly. This produces medium-rare meat with the bacon crisp. Push off onto warm plates, serving 1 skewer per person (though a few strong souls will claim they can't eat that much, they usually do).

Note: If you jam meat close together on skewers, foods cook slowly, so allow more space between meat and vegetables for well-done meats. Spear onions crosswise or diagonally, not through the centers, and mushroom caps on a diagonal.

GREEK LAMB KEBABS

Lamb grilled on pushcart charcoal firepots is a fond memory of many tourists who have visited Athens and the Greek islands. You also see Greek-style lamb kebabs sold on the streets of New York, the skewerful of meat served with a pita bread.

2 pounds lean, well-trimmed leg of lamb,
     cut in 1½-inch cubes
¼ cup each rich-flavored olive oil and lemon juice
15 to 20 bay leaves
1 teaspoon crumbled oregano
½ teaspoon salt
Freshly ground pepper to taste
2 onions, cut in wedges

Makes 6 servings.

Place lamb in a plastic bag or dish. In a small bowl combine olive oil and lemon juice, 2 bay leaves finely crumbled, the oregano, salt, and pepper. Pour over lamb, mix well, and let marinate at room temperature about 1 hour. Drain meat well, reserving marinade. Thread lamb and onion pieces on skewers, spearing a bay leaf between pieces of meat and onion here and there.

Grill 4 to 5 inches from hot coals, basting occasionally with the reserved marinade, until done as desired, about 15 minutes for medium-rare. Push meat off skewers and serve hot.

ARMENIAN SHISH KEBAB

Armenian friends in California taught me to cook vegetables on skewers separate from the meat skewers so that the vegetables don't overcook before the meat is done. They marinate the meat in very simple seasonings — red wine, olive oil, just a bit of mint, and garlic — to bring out the natural good flavor of the lamb.

3 pounds boneless leg of lamb, cut in 1½-inch cubes

½ cup dry red wine

2 tablespoons olive oil

½ teaspoon dried mint flakes, or 2 tablespoons minced
     fresh parsley

2 cloves garlic, minced

6 to 8 plum tomatoes

2 large green or sweet red peppers, quartered

2 medium onions, quartered

2 large zucchini (about 6 ounces each), each cut in
     4 chunks

Salt and freshly ground pepper

Makes 6 generous servings.

In a bowl combine lamb, wine, oil, mint or parsley, and garlic. Mix with your hands or a spoon. Cover and marinate 30 minutes at room temperature or 4 hours in refrigerator, turning once or twice. Drain lamb, reserving marinade, and thread on skewers. Thread tomatoes on other skewers, green pepper and onion pieces on other skewers, and zucchini pieces on another skewer.

Grill lamb 3 to 4 inches above hot coals for 10 minutes. Place vegetable kebabs on grill, with peppers and onions near hottest part of fire, zucchini next, and tomatoes at edge of grill. Brush meat and vegetables with reserved marinade. Turn and grill lamb until almost done, about 5 minutes longer, and push off skewers into a large pot set at edge of grill to keep lamb hot while finishing vegetables. Continue to cook and baste vegetables until done as desired. Onions and green peppers require 18 to 20 minutes, zucchini 10 minutes, and tomatoes 8 to 10 minutes.

To serve, arrange lamb cubes in center of a large platter. Push vegetables off skewers and arrange around meat for colorful display. Serve hot with pilaf or potato salad. The typical Armenian salad usually served with shish kebab includes more of the same vegetables — chopped tomato, green pepper, and onion — plus a handful of minced parsley, greens, and a lemon and oil dressing.

KOFTA KEBABS

Kofta is a fine-textured dense meatball typical of eastern Mediterranean cooking. Traditionally vigorous kneading of the meat has produced the firm texture of the meat. Although I learned from Armenian friends in California how to knead the meat by hand, I have found that a food processor not only works as well but is faster.

2 small onions, cut in chunks

2 cloves garlic, smashed

2 eggs

1 teaspoon cinnamon

1 teaspoon salt

Freshly ground pepper to taste

2 pounds ground lean lamb (see Note page 82)

Fine dry bread crumbs

Makes
5 or 6
servings.

To prepare by hand, finely chop onions and garlic and knead thoroughly into meat with eggs and seasonings. To prepare in food processor, put onions in processor fitted with steel blade and finely chop. Add garlic, eggs, cinnamon, salt, and pepper and process until well blended. Add lamb and process until pasty, once or twice turning motor off and scraping side of container. Chill well.

Gather up hunks of meat mixture about the size of golf balls, flatten, and sprinkle 1 side with bread crumbs. Shape, crumbed side in, around flat skewers and coat outside of kebabs with crumbs. Place kebabs in well-greased hinged wire grill, arranging so skewers don't slip through wires.

Grill 3 to 4 inches above hot coals until browned; turn and brown other side. Allow 10 minutes each side for well-done, 6 to 8 minutes for rare to medium. Serve on a bed of flat-leaf parsley with rice and a salad of mixed greens, finely chopped parsley, tomato, cucumber, diced sweet red and green pepper, and onion.

BARBECUED LAMB RIBS WITH PEPPERS

A *few restaurants in the West feature "Denver" ribs, actually the lamb breast trimmed of most of the surface fat and cartilage. I trim the lamb breast myself and cut the ribs in serving portions after barbecuing them. Barbecued lamb ribs have a rich, savory flavor that is complemented by herbs, garlic, and other zesty seasonings.*

4 pounds lamb breast, as lean as possible
2 cloves garlic, cut into slivers
About ½ teaspoon dried rosemary
Juice of 1 lemon
2 small green peppers, seeded and halved
2 small onions, peeled and thickly sliced

Makes 4 servings.

Trim as much surface fat as possible from lamb. Cut slits in meat and insert slivers of garlic.

Grill, curved side down, 6 inches above hot coals until browned. Turn; sprinkle with half the rosemary and half the lemon juice. Grill until browned. Move over drip pan in firebox or extinguish any flare-ups with squirts of water as lamb cooks. Turn and sprinkle with remaining rosemary and lemon juice. Arrange peppers and onions on lamb. Cook slowly until lamb is done and peppers and onions are roasted. With kitchen shears cut lamb into serving-size portions. Serve with complementary barbecue sauce (pages 129–41), lemon wedges, and vegetables.

LAMB

LAMB SHANKS WITH PINEAPPLE AND PEPPERS

Lamb shanks should be partially cooked before barbecuing to insure tenderness and remove some of the fat. The shanks can be flavored with almost any good barbecue sauce, but they are especially tasty with fresh pineapple and sweet peppers, as here.

4 small lamb shanks, ¾ pound each

Salt and freshly ground pepper

1 clove garlic, minced

1 small onion, grated or minced

½ cup oil

⅓ cup beef or chicken broth

¾ cup pineapple juice

4 thick slices fresh pineapple, peeled and cored

1 large or 2 small green peppers, seeded and quartered

Makes 4 servings.

Preheat oven to 400 degrees. Place each lamb shank on a square of aluminum foil, season lightly with salt and pepper, wrap tightly, and place in a shallow baking dish. Bake until lamb is tender, about 40 minutes. Open packets and pour off fat. Rewrap and place in a plastic food bag and refrigerate or freeze; or lamb can be cooked immediately.

Bring lamb to room temperature. In a bowl beat together garlic, onion, oil, broth, and pineapple juice. Pour into a plastic bag or dish. Unwrap lamb shanks and add, turning to coat with sauce. Marinate 1 hour at room temperature or 4 hours in refrigerator. Drain lamb, reserving marinade.

Grill lamb and pineapple 5 to 6 inches above hot coals, brushing once or twice with reserved marinade and turning to brown and cook evenly. After 15 minutes, add pepper wedges and brush with sauce. Lamb and pineapple require 25 to 30 minutes' cooking, and peppers, 10 minutes. Arrange lamb, pineapple, and peppers on a platter.

LAMBURGERS ON BUNS

1½ pounds lean ground lamb (see Note page 82)

1 clove garlic, minced

½ teaspoon salt

¼ teaspoon freshly ground pepper

1 tablespoon lemon juice

4 sandwich buns, split and toasted

Butter

Sliced tomato and onion

Makes 4 servings.

Lightly mix lamb, garlic, salt, pepper, and lemon juice. Shape into 4 patties about 1 inch thick.

Grill 3 to 4 inches above hot coals until done as desired, turning to cook evenly and prevent burning. Total cooking time for rare will be about 12 minutes; for medium, 15 minutes; and for well-done, 20 minutes.

Spread buns with butter. Place a lamb patty on the bottom half of each bun, then top with tomato, onion, and other half of bun.

GRILLED ROLLED SHOULDER OF LAMB

The trend to boneless cuts of meat has brought boned and rolled shoulder to some markets. If your meat man does not keep boned lamb shoulders in stock, he can bone, roll, and tie one for you if you order it a few days in advance. A boned and rolled shoulder is juicy and full-flavored—some think tastier than leg of lamb. It makes a compact roast that is easy to carve.

1 lamb shoulder, boned, rolled, and tied, 4 to 6 pounds

2 cups beef or chicken broth

1/4 cup soy sauce

2 cloves garlic, minced

1 tablespoon grated orange peel

Few drops hot pepper sauce

Makes 6 to 8 servings, with leftovers.

Place lamb in a plastic bag or large bowl. Mix broth, soy sauce, garlic, orange peel, and pepper sauce. Pour over lamb, turn to coat well with marinade, and marinate at room temperature 1 to 2 hours. Drain lamb, reserving marinade. Place drip pan in firebox of grill, pushing hot coals to back or around drip pan. Place lamb over drip pan.

Grill 2 to 2½ hours, until meat thermometer inserted near center registers 130 degrees for rare, 150 for medium, or 160 for well-done. Turn and baste with marinade as needed to cook evenly and prevent charring. Let stand 15 to 20 minutes before carving.

BARBECUED STUFFED BREAST OF LAMB

1 lamb breast rack, 1½ to 2 pounds
1 pound ground lean lamb
2 cloves garlic, minced
2 tablespoons minced fresh or 2 teaspoons
    dried rosemary
Salt and freshly ground pepper
Dry red wine

Makes 4 servings.

Have lamb breast cut with a pocket so it can be stuffed. Mix ground lamb with garlic, 1 teaspoon rosemary, ¼ teaspoon salt, and pepper to taste. Push lamb mixture firmly into pocket of lamb breast. This will form a compact triangle of meat with a bony side and a meaty side and ground lamb forming the longest side of the triangle. (Some markets prepare lamb breast with meat stuffing, but it will not be seasoned.) Before cooking, sprinkle remaining rosemary over lamb.

Place lamb breast bony side down about 8 inches above moderately hot coals. Have a water pistol or squirt bottle handy to extinguish any flare-ups. Sprinkle meat with red wine now and then. When bony side is browned, turn the roast to meaty side of the breast and grill until browned. By this time the ground meat filling will be firm. Turn filling down toward coals and grill until done as desired. Total grilling time for medium-rare lamb will be about 1 hour. Cut through lamb breast between bones to form triangular slices for serving. (Kitchen shears cut through bones and connective tissue more easily than a knife.)

Note: Buy 2 pounds lamb shoulder, cut out bone and most of the visible fat and sinew, and put through meat grinder or process with steel blade in food processor.

GRILLED LAMB KIDNEYS

Breakfast on the terrace or in the back yard is a joyous spring Sunday tradition. Should you awaken one morning to warm sunshine and are prepared with lamb kidneys on hand, let them become the centerpiece of your breakfast. One spring Sunday we scrambled eggs in a skillet at the edge of the grill and toasted thick slices of sourdough bread to go with the kidneys. The bread was buttered generously and served with homemade strawberry preserves. We had fresh apricots off the back yard tree for fruit.

6 to 8 lamb kidneys

2 tablespoons olive oil

1 tablespoon red wine vinegar

1/2 teaspoon thyme

1/2 teaspoon freshly ground pepper

6 slices bacon, cut in squares

Makes 6 servings, with eggs or bacon or ham accompaniments.

Wash lamb kidneys; split them and remove fat and any tough sinewy portions. Place in plastic bag; add oil, vinegar, thyme, and pepper and marinate at room temperature 10 to 15 minutes. Thread kidneys lengthwise or slightly diagonally on short skewers, placing a square of bacon between each piece.

Brush with marinade and grill 3 to 4 inches from hot fire until browned. Turn and grill other side. Slip off skewers onto warm plates and serve at once.

VICE PRESIDENT BRECKINRIDGE AT A BARBECUE

"Old Crow is present" on this and similar occasions, when such noted Kentuckians as "General John C. Breckinridge, Senator James B. Beck, Senator Joe Blackburn, or the Governor of the state," gather for a day of political oratory, roast sheep and mint juleps.*

*From the Memoirs of Henry F. Johnson.

CHICKEN, OTHER BIRDS, AND A RABBIT

Barbecuing adds character to the young, bland-flavored chickens that today's agricultural science has given us. These chickens need flavor, and smoke and piquant sauces help provide it. Young chickens cook quickly, usually in a half hour over a well-controlled fire. The modern broiler-fryer is slaughtered at about nine weeks of age (as compared to twelve to fifteen weeks a generation ago) to insure its tenderness.

We have barbecued hundreds of chickens on back yard and campfire

grills and seen thousands barbecued at huge men's club grills in Clewiston, Florida, throughout Georgia and Alabama, and on the eastern shore of Maryland, where chicken growers stage huge barbecues in the spring.

Turkey is a younger, more tender if slightly less flavorful bird than it was twenty years ago, so it, too, is often grilled successfully. In the 1960s when we moved to California, the turkey industry was promoting turkey as year-round food, and the idea seems to have taken hold. One of my summertime cooking rituals is to barbecue a turkey on the Fourth of July or on one weekend, and then to enjoy turkey salad and sandwiches the rest of the week.

Duckling and other birds benefit from wood or charcoal grilling. Duckling with ginger sauce has an exotic flavor that will be appreciated by venturesome eaters among your friends.

And rabbit! One summer evening we arrived at a friend's back yard grill in Florida as he was ceremoniously anointing what appeared to be a four-legged chicken with sauce. He joked a few minutes about "the funny chickens the butcher gave him," then said in mock horror, "You've never barbecued rabbit?" It is meaty and juicy, if you take care not to overcook it, and absorbs sauce better than chicken does, I believe. If I had to choose between rabbit and chicken for grilling, I think I would choose rabbit. Unfortunately the tender, freshly dressed young rabbits that we used to get are hard to find. But should you on a drive see a sign saying "fresh rabbits," stop and buy one, if they're young and the seller will dress them. It is heartening how many cottage-industry farmers there are in all parts of the country now supplying foods that had become almost impossible to buy. And if you don't find freshly dressed rabbits, nearly all supermarkets have or can get for you frozen rabbits.

BARBECUED CHICKEN QUARTERS

Choose any sauce you like, but my favorite is the Florida-style sauce, perhaps because I was brought up on it. Texas-style, Georgia-style, or any other style chicken is cooked the same — don't burn it, and grill it tender and juicy!

3 broiler-fryers, quartered, about 3 pounds each
Florida Barbecue Sauce (page 135)

Makes 12 medium-size or 6 very generous servings.

Place chicken, skin side down, 4 to 5 inches above hot fire. Cook 10 minutes or until skin side is browned. Turn and brown bony side. Brush *sparingly* with sauce; turn and grill 25 to 30 minutes longer, brushing thinly with sauce each time you turn the chicken, every 5 minutes or so. Serve remaining sauce on the side, with a salad or summer fruit as accompaniment.

TEXAS BARBECUED CHICKEN

Jane Cherry never lost her Texas accent or hand at barbecuing in the years that she and Heston lived in Los Angeles. They moved back to College Station, Texas, and Jane recommends this chicken, served hot or cold, with fruits for summer midday dinners in their hot area.

1 broiler-fryer, 2½ pounds, quartered
Poultry Seasoning Mix (page 131)
Texas Barbecue Sauce (page 136)

Makes 4 servings.

Rub chicken thoroughly with seasoning mix. Place chicken on grill 4 to 6 inches above coals burned down to a rosy glow. Grill until browned, turn and grill until browned on second side. This will take about 10 minutes on each side. Turn and grill until almost done, about 15 minutes longer. Brush with sauce and grill 10 minutes longer, turning once or twice and basting lightly with sauce. Heat remaining sauce and serve at table with chicken. Transfer chicken to a platter.

TWO-SAUCE CHICKEN

Chicken prepared this way turns a rich mahogany color, but does not burn if you keep extinguishing any flames with a convenient water bottle. The first sauce gives the chicken a pale tawny color; the second brings it to a reddish gold.

3 broiler-fryers, split, or 2, quartered,
    2 to 2½ pounds each
2 cups vinegar
2 teaspoons salt
3 tablespoons prepared mustard, preferably Dijon-style
3 tablespoons catsup
⅓ cup lemon juice
½ teaspoon freshly ground pepper
¼ cup sugar
5⅓ tablespoons (⅓ cup) butter, melted
1 tablespoon Worcestershire sauce

Makes 6 to 8 servings.

Place chicken in a large dish or in 2 plastic bags. Combine vinegar, 1 teaspoon salt, 1 tablespoon mustard, the catsup, lemon juice, and pepper. Pour over chicken and turn chicken in marinade. Cover and refrigerate overnight.

For second sauce combine sugar, remaining 1 teaspoon salt, butter, remaining 2 tablespoons mustard, and Worcestershire sauce. Set aside.

Remove chicken from marinade and place bony side down 4 to 6 inches above hot coals. Grill 5 minutes, turn, and baste with marinade until starting to brown, about 20 minutes. Grill 30 minutes longer, turning once or twice and basting lightly with the second sauce. Test for doneness and remove to platter. Serve hot with remaining butter sauce.

CAROLINA MUSTARD CHICKEN

For years barbecue chefs have overlooked the flavor-enforcing benefit of good broth in a basting sauce. You won't taste broth here, but the chicken will have a richer and deeper flavor.

¼ cup vegetable oil or butter
8 meaty chicken pieces (breasts, thighs, drumsticks)
1½ cups well-seasoned chicken broth
¼ cup Dijon-style mustard

Makes 4 servings.

Put oil or butter in a small saucepan that can be used on grill. Arrange chicken 4 inches above medium-hot coals; brush lightly with oil or butter, reserving what remains. Grill chicken until browned; turn, baste, and grill other side. If fire flares up, extinguish flames.

Meanwhile, stir chicken broth and mustard into oil or butter remaining in saucepan, and heat at edge of grill. Brush chicken generously with sauce and grill until tender, turning and basting as needed to cook evenly and prevent charring. This will take 30 to 45 minutes for average-size chicken pieces. Serve hot with remaining hot sauce on side.

JAPANESE–STYLE BARBECUED CHICKEN

½ cup sake or dry sherry
½ cup soy sauce
2 tablespoons honey
1 teaspoon freshly ground pepper
1 broiler-fryer, quartered, 2½ pounds

Makes 4 servings.

In a stainless-steel or enamelware saucepan combine sake or sherry, soy sauce, honey, and pepper. Simmer 15 minutes. Pour sauce over chicken in plastic bag or glass dish. Let marinate at room temperature 45 minutes or overnight in refrigerator.

Grill chicken 4 to 6 inches above hot coals, turning and brushing with marinade as needed to cook evenly and prevent charring. Serve immediately with rice and sautéed mushrooms seasoned with garlic and scallion.

BARBECUED MUSTARD CHICKEN

The flavors here could come straight from the Rhone Valley, but the chicken barbecue scheme is pure Californian—winy flavored, delicately spiced and sweetened.

1 cup dry white wine (California Chardonnay or white
    table wine)

1/2 cup olive oil

1/2 teaspoon salt

1/2 teaspoon freshly ground pepper

1 teaspoon herbes de Provence, or 1/2 teaspoon oregano

1 broiler-fryer, quartered, 3 pounds

1 tablespoon Dijon-style mustard

1 tablespoon honey

Makes 4 servings.

In a bowl beat together wine, oil, salt, pepper, and herbs or oregano. Place chicken in a bowl or plastic bag and add marinade. Marinate at room temperature 1 to 1 1/2 hours, agitating chicken now and then to coat it with the sauce. Drain chicken, reserving marinade.

Grill chicken 4 to 6 inches above hot fire, turning and basting as needed to cook evenly and prevent charring. Chicken will require 35 to 40 minutes' cooking. Combine 2 tablespoons remaining marinade with the mustard and honey. Brush over chicken and grill over coals until glazed and fragrant.

YOGURT CHICKEN

In *India chicken marinated in yogurt and spices is grilled in a tandoori oven, a cylinder-shaped stone chamber heated from below by a wood fire. This recipe, for a conventional charcoal grill, borrows the exotic seasonings of tandoori chicken. The yogurt distributes the spices through the chicken and is an effective tenderizer. Meat marinated this way will be butter-tender without being dry or mushy.*

1 cup plain yogurt

2 cloves garlic, minced

1 small onion, finely chopped

1½ teaspoons coriander seeds, cracked

1 teaspoon ground cumin

2 teaspoons turmeric

1 teaspoon minced fresh mint, or pinch dried
    mint flakes

1 broiler-fryer, quartered, 2 to 2½ pounds each

Makes 4 servings.

Mix yogurt, garlic, onion, coriander, cumin, turmeric, and mint. Place chicken in a shallow dish or plastic bag and spread with yogurt marinade. The marinade will be thick. Cover or tie bag closed and let stand at room temperature 2 to 3 hours or in refrigerator 8 to 12 hours, turning bag or chicken now and then. Scrape off loose onion and excess marinade into a small saucepan.

Grill chicken 6 to 8 inches from hot coals; brush with more marinade as needed and turn to cook evenly. Cook just until tender and golden, 40 minutes for a medium chicken.

Note: This chicken can be cooked in a kitchen. Bake the chicken at 400 degrees in a shallow baking dish, turning and basting until done, about 35 minutes.

BARBECUED CHICKEN WITH SWEET POTATOES

1/2 cup pineapple juice
1/2 cup catsup
2 tablespoons cider vinegar
1 tablespoon honey
2 or 3 dashes hot pepper sauce
1 tablespoon prepared yellow mustard
3 broiler-fryers, quartered, 2 to 2 1/2 pounds
2 to 3 tablespoons oil
6 large sweet potatoes

Makes 12 medium-size or 6 very generous servings.

Combine pineapple juice, catsup, vinegar, honey, pepper sauce, and mustard. Mix well. Place chicken in a plastic bag or shallow dish. Pour sauce over it, turn well, and marinate at room temperature 1 to 2 hours. Drain chicken well, reserving marinade.

Brush lightly with oil and grill 4 to 6 inches above hot coals until lightly browned, turning as necessary to brown evenly. Meanwhile, peel sweet potatoes and cut lengthwise in slabs about 1/2 inch thick. Place sweet potatoes on grill around chicken. Brush chicken and sweet potatoes lightly with reserved marinade. Grill, turning and basting often, until chicken is done and sweet potatoes tender, about 35 minutes. Serve hot with tossed green salad or coleslaw.

BUTTERFLIED CHICKEN WITH LEMON AND THYME

1 broiler-fryer, about 3½ pounds
1 large lemon, halved
3 sprigs fresh or ½ teaspoon dried thyme
Olive oil
Lemon wedges, fresh thyme, or parsley

*Makes 4
servings.*

Ask your butcher to butterfly a chicken for you, or do it yourself with poultry or kitchen shears and a sharp knife. Place the chicken on a cutting board or heavy paper to protect the counter. With good shears cut as close to the backbone as possible from tail to neck cavity. Cut away backbone at other side and pull it out. (The backbone, wing tips, and other trimmings can be frozen for making soup or stock.) Cut any sharp bone edges or ragged pieces of skin to smooth the edge. Flatten the chicken with the heel of your hand, then smack it hard over the breastbone, which is surrounded by translucent cartilage. Cut the filament that covers the breastbone, then turn the chicken inside out and pull out the breastbone. Butterflying the chicken allows the meat to cook evenly and makes carving neat slices easier.

Place chicken in a plastic bag and squeeze the lemon over it. Rub lemon into fleshy pieces. Sprinkle chicken with thyme. Close bag and marinate chicken at room temperature 45 minutes or in the refrigerator for several hours. Turn the bag 2 or 3 times to distribute juices and seasonings.

Remove chicken from bag and place skin side up on grill 5 inches above hot coals. Brush generously with oil and cook until browned; turn and brush with oil and cook until browned. Move chicken to edge of grill or cover grill and cook 35 minutes longer or until chicken is tender and golden brown.

Meanwhile, in a small saucepan heat 2 to 3 tablespoons oil and the remaining lemon-thyme mixture. Brush over chicken and transfer to a hot platter. Garnish with lemon wedges and fresh thyme or parsley, if available. Slice to serve.

GINGER CHICKEN

Freshly grated ginger root has a mysterious spiciness that somehow is lost in drying and grinding, so for this recipe get fresh ginger root if at all possible.

You use only a tiny piece of ginger in this and most recipes, but the remaining ginger is easy to keep. Freeze it, or keep, peeled and cut up, in a jar of sherry or vodka in the refrigerator for several weeks (it will keep this way and you can grate or slice off pieces as needed). The vodka or sherry can then be used in punches or as a flavoring for hot tea.

1/4 cup dry vermouth
1/4 cup soy sauce
1 tablespoon molasses or brown sugar
1/4 teaspoon freshly ground pepper
1 tablespoon grated ginger root, or 1 teaspoon ground
    ginger
1 broiler-fryer, quartered, 2 1/2 pounds

Makes 4 servings.

Combine vermouth, soy sauce, molasses or brown sugar, pepper, and ginger. Place chicken in marinade, turn to coat well, and marinate at room temperature 1 to 2 hours, turning once or twice. Drain well, reserving marinade. Grill chicken 4 to 5 inches above hot coals, turning and basting with marinade as needed to prevent burning and to cook evenly, until done but not dry, about 45 minutes. Test by cutting into an inside joint—juices should show no pink. Brush again with marinade, let glaze, then remove to platter and serve. This is good with rice and stir-fried snow peas or other green vegetable.

SOY–HONEY GLAZED CHICKEN BREASTS

Chicken glazed with sweet-savory sauces such as this can be broiled, but charcoal cooking enhances the flavor. Cook the chicken just until done through to prevent drying out.

2 chicken breasts, split, 1 pound each

1/4 cup minced scallions

2 cloves garlic, pressed

1 tablespoon honey

2 tablespoons dry sherry

2 teaspoons grated fresh ginger root (optional)

1/2 cup soy sauce

Makes 4 servings.

Skin chicken breast pieces. Combine scallions, garlic, honey, sherry, ginger root, and soy sauce. Dip chicken in sauce, then place in plastic bag and pour in remaining sauce. Close bag and marinate at room temperature 30 minutes to 1 hour.

Grill 4 inches above hot coals, turning as needed to prevent charring and to cook evenly. Grill until just done, about 25 minutes. Brush with sauce as needed to keep moist. Heat any remaining sauce and serve with chicken and hot cooked rice.

WHITE LEGHORNS,
Bred by C. A. Pitkin, Hartford, Conn.

CHICKEN

YAKITORI

Excellent!

1/99

Boneless chicken on small bamboo skewers—Japanese yakitori—goes as fast as party snacks. A serving as a main dish is two of the little skewers.

3 whole chicken breasts, halved, skinned, boned, and
    cut in 1-inch cubes
1/2 cup sake or dry sherry
1/2 cup soy sauce
1 tablespoon sugar
1 clove garlic, smashed
2 green or sweet red peppers, cut in cubes
1 medium onion, cut in 8 wedges

Makes 12 appetizer servings; 4 to 6 main-dish servings.

Place chicken in a shallow dish or plastic bag. Mix sake or sherry, soy sauce, sugar, and garlic. Pour over chicken, turn to coat chicken well, cover, and refrigerate 2 to 3 hours. Drain marinade into a small saucepan and heat at edge of grill while fire is burning down. Thread chicken pieces, pepper cubes, and onion pieces on bamboo skewers that have been soaked in cold water to prevent charring. Spear onion pieces diagonally through outer layer so that pieces will not fall off while cooking.

Grill on a hibachi or 2 or 3 inches from hot fire, turning once or twice. Total grilling time will be about 4 minutes.

TANGY BARBECUED CHICKEN PIECES

Some markets in New York City offer a shaker jar of seasoning called "adobo." It is used liberally in Puerto Rican cooking, a friend told me, as a dry mix to rub on meats. I sometimes use it in this recipe instead of the salt, garlic, oregano, paprika, and lemon juice.

1 teaspoon salt

1 clove garlic, peeled, plus 2 cloves, minced

1½ teaspoons oregano

¼ teaspoon paprika

1 tablespoon lemon juice

8 meaty chicken pieces (breasts, thighs, drumsticks)

3 tablespoons oil

1 small onion, minced

⅓ cup catsup

⅓ cup cider vinegar

Makes 4 servings.

In a mortar and pestle or bowl with back of a spoon, mash salt with peeled clove garlic until almost a paste. Mash in ½ teaspoon oregano, paprika, and lemon juice. Rub this mixture over chicken. Brush with 1 tablespoon oil.

Grill 4 to 5 inches above hot coals, turning as needed to cook evenly and prevent charring. Meanwhile, in a small saucepan at edge of grill sauté onion in remaining 2 tablespoons oil until tender. Add minced garlic and sauté a few seconds. Stir in catsup, vinegar, and remaining oregano and simmer 15 minutes. When chicken is done brush with sauce and grill 5 minutes longer. Pile onto a warm platter and serve remaining sauce at table.

CHICKEN THIGHS WITH PESTO

Fresh basil has become a national passion and is available from most greengrocers. It grows in many an herb bed, and a friend who lives in a New York apartment has it in a pot on her bedroom windowsill. One night I had some leftover pesto and I tried it as a sauce for grilled chicken thighs.

Chicken thighs are first choice for barbecuing because they are meaty and juicier than other chicken parts. The pesto contributes a rich herby flavor that makes this a savory dish, especially when accompanied by rice cooked in chicken broth and a big green salad tossed with an olive oil and balsamic vinegar dressing.

⅓ cup oil

⅓ cup Pesto (recipe follows)

12 chicken thighs

Additional Pesto

Makes 6 servings.

In a shallow dish combine oil and pesto, beating with fork until well mixed. Dip chicken thighs in sauce, turn, and cover. Let stand at room temperature 30 minutes.

Grill chicken 3 to 4 inches above hot coals, basting once or twice with sauce. Cook and turn until done, about 35 minutes. Heat remaining sauce to serve with chicken at table. Pass additional Pesto, at room temperature, if you wish.

PESTO

2 cups fresh basil leaves, loosely packed

2 cloves garlic, smashed

¼ cup walnuts or pine nuts

½ to ¾ cup olive oil

½ cup freshly grated Parmesan cheese

¼ teaspoon salt, or to taste

Makes about 1 cup.

In a blender or processor combine basil, garlic, nuts, and ½ cup oil. Process until almost smooth. If pasty, add more oil. Scrape into a bowl and beat in cheese and salt to taste. Serve as a sauce on pasta or rice or use as a flavoring for vegetable soup, as well as in sauce for Chicken Thighs with Pesto.

GRILLED CHICKEN GIBLETS

Chicken giblets grilled as hors d'oeuvres are snatched almost as fast as you can cook them so you might want to ask a helper to keep up with the demand for giblets while you get the main meat done.

½ teaspoon salt

½ teaspoon freshly ground pepper

½ teaspoon sugar

½ teaspoon dried leaf sage

2 tablespoons wine vinegar or lemon juice

⅓ cup olive oil

Livers, hearts, and gizzards from 3 broiler-fryers

Makes a few bites each for 6 persons.

In a small bowl mix salt, pepper, sugar, and sage. Stir in vinegar or juice until seasonings are well mixed. Add oil and beat until well blended. Let stand while preparing giblets. Rinse giblets and cut away any cartilage or fat. Cut large gizzards and livers in half. Place giblets in plastic bag and add sauce. Close bag tightly and turn to coat giblets with sauce. Have a square of wire cloth or a fine-mesh cake rack on grill so that giblets don't fall through wide slats.

Remove giblets from marinade and place on screen or cake rack. Cook until crispy but not overcooked, spear on wood picks, and serve immediately. Pieces of liver take about 3 minutes; the hearts, 4 to 5 minutes; and the gizzards, 5 to 7 minutes.

CHICKEN LIVER KEBABS

Grilled chicken livers are good any time, but miniature skewers of them make fine hors d'oeuvres with drinks before the main meal.

1½ pounds chicken livers

2 tablespoons oil, plus additional oil for basting

1 tablespoon soy sauce

1 tablespoon dry red wine or chicken broth

¼ teaspoon freshly ground pepper

¼ teaspoon dried or 1 teaspoon minced fresh marjoram

12 pieces scallions, cut in 2-inch lengths

12 mushroom caps

Boiling water

Makes 4 to 6 generous servings.

Pick over chicken livers and discard any discolored ones. Cut large livers in half. Place livers in a bowl. Sprinkle with 2 tablespoons oil, soy sauce, wine or broth, pepper, and marjoram. Mix well, cover, and refrigerate 30 minutes. Blanch vegetables to prevent splitting when threading them on skewers: place scallions and mushrooms in separate bowls, cover with boiling water, and let stand 10 to 15 minutes.

Thread chicken livers, scallion pieces, and mushrooms on skewers, alternating so that meat and vegetable juices will blend while grilling. Brush lightly with oil and grill 4 inches above hot fire, turning and brushing lightly with oil to cook evenly. Livers will require about 10 to 12 minutes to become crispy-coated and pink and tender inside. Avoid overcooking as livers become tough and dry. Serve hot with rice or potatoes.

SPIT-ROASTED CORNISH HENS

Look for the smallest game hens — 1¹/4 pounds, if possible. Four roasting on a spit look festive and sumptuous. Keep them well buttered so that they come out moist and flavorful.

4 Cornish game hens, thawed if frozen
Salt and freshly ground pepper
Butter, softened

Makes 4 large servings.

Season cavities of birds with salt and pepper. Tie drumsticks to tails and wrap twine around breasts to hold wings in place. Push spit through birds from neck skin through the body and out just above tail. Fasten securely with spit forks. Rub birds heavily with butter.

Engage spit and start turning over drip pan. Baste with additional butter to keep moist. Hens weighing 1½ pounds require 45 minutes' to 1 hour's cooking. Remove birds from spit and serve 1 to a person or split and serve half to a person. Pass flavored butter of your choice (see pages 142–4).

OTHER BIRDS

GRILLED TURKEY CUTLETS

Years ago, before turkey breast cutlets were generally available in super-markets, we often mystified our friends with these wing-shaped steaks. We would ask Leon, our butcher, to saw cutlets from the breast portion of a hard-frozen turkey. He would put the turkey on the electric meat saw and cut 1/2-inch steaks from just below the wing down to the lower part of the breast. We would save the hind part of the turkey and the wings for other dishes. Now turkey cutlets are in most markets and often are used as a substitute for veal cutlets.

4 to 6 turkey cutlets, 4 ounces each

1 cup oil

1/2 cup dry white wine

2 teaspoons minced fresh or 1/8 teaspoon rubbed sage

Salt and freshly ground pepper

Makes 4 to 6 servings.

Place turkey in a shallow dish and pour oil and wine over it. Sprinkle with sage. Marinate at room temperature 1 hour or in the refrigerator for 3 to 4 hours, turning 2 or 3 times. Bring dish to grill. Remove each turkey cutlet from marinade and let drip into dish.

Place on well-greased grill about 4 inches above hot fire. Grill, turning and basting as needed for even cooking, about 15 minutes, until turkey is done through but not dry. Serve with Lemon Butter (see page 142) or a fruit relish or chutney.

SPIT–BARBECUED TURKEY

Barbecued turkey was in high fashion when we moved to California in 1960. We arrived at the first four or five dinner parties to which we were invited to find the hosts watching over turkeys turning slowly on spits over charcoal fires. It can be a culinary triumph, juicy and flavorful with sauce. I still prefer the sharp and acidy barbecue sauce that we used on chicken in Florida, but some people like fruity sauces and others like Carolina-style sauces.

1 turkey, 10 to 12 pounds

Barbecue sauce of your choice (pages 129–41)

Makes 10 to 12 servings, with leftovers.

Check clearance between spit and grill and the circumference of turkey before buying it, but a 12-pound bird will turn smoothly on most grills equipped with spits. Brush inside of turkey lightly with barbecue sauce. Run spit from center of neck skin through body and out just above the tail. Fasten tightly with spit forks. Tie wings to turkey with twine and tie legs and tail together below spit rod. Roll spit rod in palms to check the balance.

Place drip pan under spot where spit will turn and push hot coals to back or side. Engage spit, start motor, and grill turkey until skin is blistered and browned. Raise spit so that turkey turns about 7 inches above coals or poke coals to edge, leaving a thin layer to provide moderate heat. Continue grilling and basting turkey. As drippings collect in drip pan, carefully pour into sauce. Grill turkey until internal temperature registers 180 degrees on meat thermometer, 2½ to 3 hours for a 10- to 12-pound turkey. Cut strings and let turkey rest 20 minutes before carving.

TURKEY BREAST VERMILION

2 tablespoons brown sugar

1 tablespoon prepared mustard

½ cup each orange juice and catsup

1 turkey breast, bone in, 5½ pounds

Oil (optional)

Makes 6 to 8 servings, with leftovers.

Combine brown sugar, mustard, orange juice, and catsup. Beat together until sugar is dissolved and sauce well mixed. Place turkey in a plastic food bag and pour in sauce. Close bag tightly and turn to coat turkey with sauce. Place in a dish and refrigerate 6 to 8 hours, turning several times to coat turkey.

Place a drip pan in firebox of grill, arranging coals around pan or at one end and placing pan at the other. Carefully remove turkey from sauce, reserving sauce.

Place turkey on grill about 6 inches above hot coals. Grill, turning as needed, and brown on all sides, about 15 minutes. Move turkey over drip pan. Cover grill or tuck a loose tent of foil around turkey to hold in heat. Roast slowly, basting with drippings or oil now and then and turning to cook evenly. Roast to an internal temperature of 160 degrees, thoroughly done but still moist. This will require about 2 hours. Let turkey stand 20 minutes before carving. Meanwhile, heat sauce. Thinly slice turkey and serve with warm sauce.

SMOKY GINGER DUCKLING

Generally, I don't like precooking meat before barbecuing it, but this method rids duck of some of the excessive fat. The elegant dish is worth it and you avoid dangerous flare-ups and messy clean-up.

1 duckling, 4 to 5 pounds

2 or 3 thin slices fresh ginger root, cut in fine shreds,
    plus additional sliced ginger for garnish

2 tablespoons duck drippings

2 cloves garlic, minced

½ cup orange juice

Roasted Orange Halves (page 183)

Makes 4 small or 2 large servings.

I prefer fresh duckling, but if using frozen thaw it thoroughly in refrigerator. Clip off wing tips, remove neck and giblets, and freeze for other uses. Preheat oven to 400 degrees. Place duckling breast side up in a shallow pan on rack and roast 1 hour. Puncture skin with fork in several places to allow fat to cook out, turn duckling back side up, and roast 30 minutes longer or until juices in cavity lose their red color. Cool duckling until it can be handled. With poultry or kitchen shears cut out backbone. Cut duckling in half along breastbone. Working with small knife and fingers, pull rib cages from each half of duck. Sprinkle cavities with shredded ginger. In a small saucepan heat the 2 tablespoons duck drippings, add garlic, and cook until golden. Stir in orange juice and heat slightly.

Place duckling halves skin side down over drip pan surrounded by hot coals or with hot coals at back. Turn and baste duckling with sauce. Close grill cover or tuck a loose tent of foil around duck to hold in heat. Grill 45 minutes or until meat is juicy, skin browned and crispy, and duck done. Remove to platter and garnish with more ginger and Roasted Orange Halves.

SPIT–ROASTED DUCKLING

½ cup orange marmalade
¼ cup wine vinegar
1 teaspoon Dijon-style mustard
1 small onion, minced
1 duckling, 5 to 6 pounds

Makes 2 large or 4 moderate servings.

Combine marmalade, vinegar, and mustard. Stir in onion until sauce is blended. When fire has burned down to glowing coals, place drip pan in firebox with coals pushed to back and drip pan under area where spit will turn. Run spit through duck from center of neck skin through body and out just above the tail. Fasten firmly with spit forks. Tie wings to body around breast and legs together at tail, using kitchen twine.

Engage spit and start motor. Brush duck lightly with sauce. Roast duck 2 hours without basting, as fat serves as a natural basting. As drip pan fills with drippings, remove some of the fat with a bulb baster and put in a container for discarding, your hands protected with heavy barbecue mitts to avoid danger of fire. In last 30 minutes baste duckling 2 or 3 times with sauce. Remove duck to platter and let stand 20 minutes before carving. Serve with remaining sauce and, if desired, Roasted Orange Halves (see page 183).

BARBECUED RABBIT

Rabbit grills meaty and tender, the firm white meat absorbing any sauce you baste it with to point up the mild flavor.

2 fresh-dressed or thawed frozen rabbits, 2½ pounds
    each
Florida Barbecue Sauce (page 135)

Makes 8 generous servings.

Cut rabbit in halves or quarters. Place meaty side down on grill 5 to 6 inches above hot coals, baste lightly with sauce, and grill until browned, about 10 minutes. Turn and baste lightly. Continue grilling, turning, and basting as needed to cook evenly and prevent charring, about 45 minutes. Make a deep slit into a thigh joint; if juices run clear, rabbit is done. If juice is pink, grill rabbit 10 to 15 minutes longer. Remove rabbit to a warm platter. Serve a quarter to each person, or carve halves in pieces: 2 legs and 2 to 4 body portions per half rabbit. Serve remaining sauce on the side and provide plenty of paper napkins as diners will like to gnaw the bones.

FISH AND SEAFOOD

Barbecuing fish is a great American culinary tradition. Indians grilled fish over wood fires long before European settlers arrived. One summer evening in 1981 thirty of us took a motor launch from Seattle to an island in Puget Sound for grilled salmon. A young man was tending an alder wood fire, turning the fat sides of salmon as Indians have for several hundred years. When we ate the salmon it was pleasantly smoky-flavored and juicy. In Florida, I've seen Seminoles roast whole fish at the edge of a campfire. Some historians believe that early settlers in Savannah learned to roast oysters from Indians, but in any case diaries of settlers recorded oyster

roasts as a social diversion within a few months after the arrival of the first colonists in 1733.

No fish tastes so good as one caught, cleaned, and cooked on the spot. When we fished the canals and lakes of south Florida, a small barbecue grill and bag of charcoal were stowed in the car with the fishing gear for an excursion. Fishing trip cooking was very basic—the cleaned fish put on the grill over hot coals, seasoned lightly with salt and lime or lemon brought from home, and cooked eight to ten minutes, plenty of time for small fish or fillets.

Fish is naturally tender and needs only enough cooking to set the juices. Overcooking makes fish dry and tasteless, so learn to stick a knife tip or fork in a thick section and recognize fish that is done. The flesh will lose its rather transparent appearance and look opaque, but not dry. If it is flaky, the flakes will look moist and juicy.

The recipes in this section are more elaborate than our fishing hole cookery, but still reflect my feeling that seasonings for barbecued fish be light to allow the smoky fragrance to accent the freshness of the fish. I like less pungent wood smokes with fish—fruit wood, a few twigs of hickory, or, in Florida, a small brush of Australian pine put on the fire just before the fish is finished. Mesquite, which some people use with fish, is too sharp-flavored for me.

Top-quality, well-handled fish is juicy, tender, and charmingly "fishy" when the marinade is designed to accent but not overwhelm the pure fresh flavor of fish and the fire built hot but not too pungent.

BARBECUED FISH WITH FENNEL

Fennel softens the flavor of strong-flavored fish such as mackerel and enhances the flavor of bland-flavored fish such as sea bass. Here thick slices of fennel also help keep fish from sticking to the grill. Salmon, cod, and flounder are good this way, too.

1 whole fish, cleaned and head cut off, 3 to 7 pounds
1 large head fennel
Juice of 1 lemon
Melted butter
Lemon wedges

*Makes
6 to 12
servings.*

Leave skin on fish and have it split almost through and the long backbone removed. Slice fennel, including outside stalks, as they will go on the grill. Fill fish with tender inside slices of fennel. Skewer the fish closed over fennel and tie, if necessary. Grease grill thoroughly.

When fire is hot enough to cook, place outer fennel slices on grill to serve as a bed for fish. Place fish on fennel on barbecue grill, sprinkle with lemon juice, and brush generously with butter. (Or fish and fennel can be placed in hinged wire grill.) Cover grill or shape a loose tent of aluminum foil over fish. Grill 15 minutes. Brush with butter and turn fish. Continue cooking, turning, and basting to cook evenly until fish flakes easily with a fork, about 40 minutes total for a 3-pound fish and up to 1 hour for a 7-pound fish. Place fish on warm platter, carefully lifting it from grill. (Discard fennel. It will be scorched.) Pull off skin from top with fingers, loosening it with a fork. Garnish with fresh fennel leaves and lemon wedges and serve with more melted butter.

BARBECUED WHOLE FISH

A *whole fish makes a splendid display, set on its platter with parsley or watercress and lemon wedges.*

1 firm-fleshed white-meated fish (red snapper, Pacific rock cod, or sea bass), cleaned with head left on, 2½ pounds	*Makes 4 to 6 servings.*

Salt and freshly ground pepper
½ cup oil
Fresh thyme, rosemary, or dill
2 tablespoons lemon juice
1 stick (½ cup) melted butter or Anchovy or Sage
      butter (pages 142–3)

Sprinkle fish lightly with salt and pepper. Beat together oil, 2 tablespoons minced herb, and lemon juice. Liberally brush inside and outside of fish. Rub grill heavily with oil.

Place fish in hinged wire grill or put it directly on the barbecue grill 5 to 6 inches above hot coals and close cover or shape a loose tent of foil over fish to hold in heat. Grill about 7 minutes, until lightly browned. Brush again with oil mixture, carefully turn fish, using 2 spatulas, close grill, and cook fish 7 to 8 minutes longer or until fish flakes with a fork. Just before fish is done add fresh herb sprigs to fire for added aroma. Remove fish carefully to platter and brush with remaining oil mixture. Serve with melted butter or Anchovy or Sage butter sauce.

BARBECUED CATCH OF THE DAY

Any small fish can be cooked this way, even a half-pound bluegill, but watch the small thin fish carefully so that they don't overcook. When fish is opaque at the thickest part, it is ready to serve.

4 schoolboy snappers, bluefish, walleyed pike, rockfish,
    brook trout, or sea bass, 1 pound each
½ stick (¼ cup) butter
¼ cup oil
2 tablespoons lemon or orange juice
Salt and freshly ground pepper
Lemon wedges

Makes 4 servings.

Have fish cleaned; fish is juicier if cooked with the head on, but cut it off if you insist. Thoroughly grease a hinged wire grill, as fish can stick. Arrange fish in grill so they are not quite touching. Close and fasten the grill.

Place 3 to 4 inches above hot coals. In a small saucepan, heat butter and oil. Stir in juice and brush generously on fish. Grill until browned, then turn and baste. Cook a total of 15 to 20 minutes or just until fish looks opaque when tested with a fork. Season with salt and pepper, then remove fish carefully to a platter and serve with lemon wedges.

FISH FILLETS IN ORANGE SAUCE

7/88 OK. — N. F.

Californians marinate fish this way before barbecuing it, and you'll find similar seasonings for fish in Spain and northern Africa.*

2 pounds fish fillets (snapper, cod, sea bass, monkfish)
¾ cup orange juice
1 teaspoon grated orange peel
¼ cup each oil and dry vermouth
½ teaspoon salt
Freshly ground pepper to taste
2 cloves garlic, minced
Lemon wedges

Makes 4 to 6 servings.

Place fish in a shallow dish. Combine orange juice and peel, oil, vermouth, salt, pepper, and garlic. Pour over fish and marinate 30 minutes at room temperature. Drain fish and place in a well-greased hinged wire grill or grease barbecue grill liberally.

Grill fish 3 to 4 inches above hot coals 12 to 15 minutes, just until fish flakes when tested with a fork. Remove fish to platter and garnish with lemon wedges. Serve tartar sauce, too, if desired.

GRILLED SPANISH MACKEREL FILLETS

Steve Trumbull, who considered fishing holes part of his beat at the Miami Herald, cooked mackerel this way. Jane, his wife, made the most fabulous tartar sauce you'll ever taste.

4 fresh-caught Spanish mackerel, about 1½ pounds each

Juice of 1 or 2 limes

Salt, freshly ground pepper, and dill weed

Oil

Jane Trumbull's Tartar Sauce (page 145)

Lime wedges

Makes 4 servings.

Have fish cleaned and filleted. (Doing this at the dock saves a lot of muss at home.) Wrap fillets in plastic wrap or tightly in waxed paper and keep very cold until an hour before cooking. Spread fillets flesh side up on a sheet of waxed paper. Sprinkle generously with lime juice, cutting another lime if needed. Sprinkle lightly with salt, pepper, and dill weed. Oil grill thoroughly or place fish in a well-oiled hinged grill.

Grill fish skin side down 4 inches above hot coals until skin is blistered and browned. Brush with oil, turn, and grill 7 to 10 minutes, until fish flakes with a fork. Serve hot with tartar sauce and lime wedges.

GRILLED FISH FILLETS WITH GINGER–SOY SAUCE

4/89

1/4 cup sweet sherry ⟶ 1/4 c. white Zinfandel

1/4 cup soy sauce

1 tablespoon sugar

1 tablespoon grated fresh ginger root

1 large clove garlic, minced

2 fillets salmon (tail piece) or sea bass, 1½ pounds each

Oil

Makes 4 to 6 servings.

marinate chunks of tuna & use shish-ka-bob

wonderful!

Combine sherry, soy sauce, sugar, ginger, and garlic. Mix well. Pour over fish in a shallow dish or plastic bag. Turn fish in sauce or turn bag to coat fish well. Marinate at room temperature 30 minutes or in refrigerator for several hours, turning 2 or 3 times. Remove fish from marinade and pour marinade into a small saucepan. Brush fish well with oil. Place in hinged wire grill that has been well greased and fasten shut.

Grill 3 to 4 inches above hot coals, basting with marinade and turning as needed. Grill just until fish flakes, 12 to 15 minutes. Remove to platter and serve heated sauce on side.

TURKISH–STYLE SWORDFISH KEBABS

2 swordfish or mako shark steaks, 1 inch thick, about
    2 pounds total
½ teaspoon paprika
2 tablespoons olive oil
1 tablespoon grated onion
10 to 12 bay leaves
Juice of 1 lemon
1 tablespoon finely chopped fresh parsley, preferably
    flat-leaf
½ teaspoon salt
Lemon wedges

Makes 6 servings.

Cut swordfish or mako shark in 1-inch cubes, discarding skin and bone. In a plastic bag or bowl combine fish, paprika, 1 tablespoon oil, onion, and bay leaves. Cover tightly and refrigerate 2 to 3 hours. Thread fish on skewers, spearing a bay leaf between fish cubes at intervals.

Grill 3 to 4 inches above hot fire, turning to cook evenly, until fish is cooked through but not dry, about 12 minutes. Meanwhile, beat together remaining tablespoon oil, lemon juice, parsley, and salt. Push fish off skewers onto platter and discard bay leaves. Garnish with lemon wedges and serve with sauce.

CHARCOAL–GRILLED HALIBUT OR OTHER FISH STEAKS

4 to 6 halibut, snapper, or codfish steaks,
    about 1 inch thick
¼ cup lemon juice
½ cup oil
Salt and freshly ground pepper
¼ cup minced fresh parsley, or 1 tablespoon minced
    fresh tarragon
1 tablespoon minced onion
Lemon wedges

Makes
4 to 6
servings.

Place fish in a shallow dish. Combine lemon juice, oil, salt and pepper to taste, parsley or tarragon, and onion. Pour over fish; cover and marinate at room temperature 30 minutes. Place fish in a hinged wire grill to facilitate turning or grease grill well.

Place fish 3 to 4 inches above hot coals. Grill 5 to 6 minutes on each side or until fish flakes easily when tested with a fork near the centers of steaks. Do not overcook. Serve with lemon wedges on the side.

FISH GRILLED OVER VINE CUTTINGS

W*e first had fish grilled this way at Château Canon in St.-Émilion one April when driving through Bordeaux. Wine grapevines are pruned each autumn and the cuttings are dried and saved for burning. As we drove into the broad graveled parking space at the entry of the château, a rosy-cheeked girl was tending the fish as it grilled over a tiny fire set in a garage, since a light rain was falling.*

1 sea bass, cleaned, about 3 pounds
Salt and freshly ground pepper
2 or 3 sprigs fresh tarragon
Melted butter
Vine cuttings or other small sweet wood twigs
Lemon wedges and parsley

*Makes
6 to 8
servings.*

A fish-shaped basket with short legs is ideal for grilling fish over dried vine cuttings. If you don't have a fish grill, build the fire in a small barbecue grill. Season fish cavity and skin with salt and pepper. Place tarragon sprigs in cavity and skewer fish closed. Place in basket. Brush generously with butter. Choose a smooth stone or level ground (the cement floor of an open carriage house held the fish grill that we observed in Bordeaux) for the fish grill. Vine cuttings burn fast, so have plenty of them to replenish fire as needed.

Lay the fire in an oval a little longer than the fish grill, ignite it, and when very hot place fish grill slightly to the leeward side of the fire. Grill the fish, flipping the basket to turn the fish as it browns and cooks and basting with more butter. Feed the fire as needed to keep it hot. Fish is done when it flakes with a fork. This will take about 20 minutes if fish is turned carefully and fire is kept burning furiously. Place fish on platter and garnish with lemon wedges and parsley. Serve with more melted butter.

FISH BAKED IN TI LEAVES

Mahimahi (dolphin fish) is classic for this method of grilling fish, but *any white-fleshed fish stays moist in the leaves. Ti leaves can be purchased from a florist. Banana leaves, other large edible leaves, or aluminum foil can be substituted.*

1½ pounds fish fillets or a 2½-pound whole fish,
     cleaned (mahimahi, halibut, snapper, monkfish)
Sea salt or ice cream salt
2 or 3 slices bacon, diced
1 small onion, chopped
1 bay leaf, crumbled

Makes 6 to 8 servings.

Rub fish on all sides with salt. Place on ti leaves, overlapping them to form a leakproof package. Sprinkle with bacon, onion, and bay leaf. Wrap leaves around fish and tie with a stem of ti leaf or kitchen twine.

Place fish packet on grill 3 to 4 inches above hot coals. Cook, turning as needed to cook evenly, until fish flakes easily with a fork, 30 to 45 minutes for whole fish, 15 to 20 minutes for fish fillet. Arrange fresh leaves on a platter, cutting away wilted or soiled leaves, and place fish atop.

GRILLED WHOLE SALMON IN FOIL

A *cradle of foil facilitates turning fish on a grill and prevents sticking. A fish-shaped rack of the right size for the fish works as well, but the same size rack and fish are hard to coordinate. The foil is left open to allow the smoky aroma to penetrate.*

Oil or butter

1 whole salmon, cleaned, 2½ to 3 pounds

Salt and freshly ground pepper

Juice of 1 lemon

1 tablespoon oil

3 or 4 sprigs fresh dill, plus ¼ cup chopped fresh dill

1 teaspoon Dijon-style mustard

½ stick (¼ cup) butter, softened

Lemon wedges

Makes 6 servings.

Tear off a sheet of heavy-duty foil long enough to cradle fish and leave end for turning. Poke holes at intervals in foil, using a pencil or ice pick, to allow smoke to waft through foil. Grease foil heavily with oil or soft butter. Place fish on foil. Season cavity with salt, pepper, lemon juice, and 1 tablespoon oil. Place dill sprigs in cavity and let stand at room temperature 20 minutes.

Place fish in foil on grill 4 to 5 inches above hot fire. Grill 5 minutes and with a wide spatula and tongs, carefully turn fish in foil. Grill 5 minutes and turn again. Continue grilling, turning to cook evenly, until fish flakes with fork at thickest part. Salmon requires 25 to 30 minutes' total cooking time.

Meanwhile, beat together chopped dill, mustard, and butter. Carefully lift foil off grill and roll fish onto platter. Garnish with lemon wedges and serve dill-butter sauce on side.

GRILLED LOBSTER TAILS

One summer, sailing from Miami to the Bahamas, we anchored in a sheltered cove on a stormy evening. Within a few minutes a smack boat, the favorite Bahamian fishing boat at that time, appeared as if from nowhere. The fishermen wanted to barter freshly caught rock lobster for cigarettes. We negotiated a trade, to our great delight, and grilled the tails over a brazier set in the dinghy that night. One of the cardinal rules of carefree sailing is fire prevention. Thus our charcoal fire was set in the dinghy so it could be cut loose in case it should get out of control, though in our years of sailing we never had a mishap. Grilled lobster tails make an impressive back yard barbecue for guests, and I had lobster tails grilled over a fire seasoned with mesquite chips in a restaurant on Mission Bay in San Diego only a few days before setting down this method of cooking that we have enjoyed for years.

> 1 or 2 lobster tails, about 7 ounces each, per person
> Butter or oil
> Lemon or lime wedges
> Salt and freshly ground pepper
> Melted butter or Anchovy or Green butter
>   (pages 142 and 144)

Thaw lobster tails if frozen. For a "piggyback lobster tail," cut the shell down the back lengthwise, using poultry shears or kitchen shears and leaving tail fan intact. Do not remove undershell. With fingers, pull lobster meat through the slit. Brush heavily with butter or oil and sprinkle lightly with lemon or lime juice. Grill meat side down 4 to 5 inches above hot coals until meat is opaque but still tender, about 7 minutes. Serve hot with melted butter or Anchovy or Green butter sauce.

For a "fan-cut lobster tail," snip away undershell and small legs, using shears. Snap tail back hard to break it and release the shell ligaments that tighten while cooking. Or spear the tail end to end with a skewer to keep it from curling while cooking. Spread heavily with butter or oil and sprinkle with lemon or lime juice. Grill shell side down 4 to 5 inches above hot coals about 4 minutes, until shell is brown. Brush again with oil or butter, turn flesh side down and grill 3 minutes or until meat is opaque but still tender. Serve with melted butter or Anchovy or Green butter sauce.

OYSTER ROAST

Soon after the first settlers arrived in Savannah in 1733, oyster roasts along the riverbank were a favorite entertainment. The setting is romantic—tidal marshes with cypress trees swagged in Spanish moss, camellias in bloom in the late winter, when oyster roasts are most frequent and oysters are at their plumpest and most sweetly flavored. If you're a guest in Savannah, Fernandina Beach in north Florida, or Cumberland Island, almost on the state line today, you're sure to be invited to an oyster roast, sometimes transported by boat to the site of the smoky fire and the bushels of oysters.

Oysters in the shell, at least 12 per person
Salt and freshly ground pepper
Melted butter
Lemon or lime wedges
Hot pepper sauce

Wash oysters. For easier handling grill can be covered with a sheet of heavy-duty foil with holes poked in it or a sheet of metal (the professional roasters use sheet metal), but oysters can be roasted directly on the grill.

Place oysters about 4 inches above hot coals. Cover with grill hood or with a loose tent of foil to hold in heat. When oyster shells open, in about 6 minutes, they are done. Arrange on plates, deepest half of shell down, and serve as they come off fire. Each person seasons his oysters to taste with salt and pepper and dips them in butter with lemon or lime juice and hot pepper sauce. Continue cooking oysters until nobody wants more. The classic accompaniments to the oysters are French fries or potato chips, bread, and coleslaw.

GRILLED CLAMS OREGANATE

24 clams in the shell

3 large cloves garlic, minced

1/4 cup minced fresh or 1 tablespoon dried oregano

2 tablespoons minced parsley

1 cup fine dry bread crumbs

2 tablespoons oil

Makes 6 appetizer servings or 2 main-dish servings.

Scrub clams thoroughly and discard any that are not live. Hardshells close their shells when tapped if they are live, siphon clams constrict their necks.

Place clams on grill 3 to 5 inches above hot coals. In a small skillet combine garlic, oregano, parsley, bread crumbs, and oil. Stir together to form a crumbly mixture and heat at the edge of the grill while clams are roasting. When clam shells open (after about 5 minutes), lift off top shells using mitts to protect your hands. Drop a spoonful of the herbed crumbs on each clam and heat a minute or 2. Serve at once.

CLAMS STEAMED IN FOIL

This way of steaming clams provides a miniclambake without digging a hole in the sand. If the grill is large enough, grill corn with the clams.

3 dozen littleneck clams

1 small onion, minced

1 stick (½ cup) butter

2 tablespoons minced fresh parsley

2 cloves garlic, minced

2 tablespoons lemon juice

Freshly ground pepper to taste

Makes 6 servings.

Scrub clams thoroughly with a stiff brush and discard any clams with cracked or open shells. Tear off 6 large squares of heavy-duty aluminum foil and place 6 clams in the center of each square of foil. Sprinkle with onion. Melt butter and stir in parsley, garlic, lemon juice, and pepper. Divide among the clams. Fold foil packets tightly closed at top.

Place packets 4 to 6 inches over hot coals, closed sides up. Grill 7 to 10 minutes, shaking packets and changing positions from outer edge of grill to center to let clams cook evenly. Clams will open when done. Place each foil packet in a large soup bowl and let diners open their own. Provide soup spoons for the clam broth and cocktail forks for extracting the clams.

GRILLED SHRIMP WITH BACON

Buy the largest shrimp you can find for this dish, as peeling tiny shrimp is a chore and tiny shrimp cook dry before you know it.

2 pounds jumbo shrimp
1/2 teaspoon salt
1/4 cup lemon juice
1/4 cup catsup
3 dashes hot pepper sauce
1 clove garlic, crushed
1/2 cup oil
1/2 pound sliced bacon
Lemon wedges

Makes 4 to 6 servings.

Shell and clean uncooked shrimp. In a bowl mix salt, lemon juice, catsup, pepper sauce, garlic, and oil. Marinate shrimp in mixture 30 minutes to 1 hour at room temperature. Cut each bacon slice crosswise into 4 or 5 pieces. Remove shrimp from marinade, reserving the sauce. Thread shrimp and bacon pieces alternately on skewers, leaving space between to allow heat to penetrate.

Grill 3 to 4 inches above hot coals just until shrimp is opaque and bacon is crisp, 8 to 10 minutes. Turn several times while grilling to cook evenly and brush each time with the reserved sauce. Bacon drippings make fire flare up, so keep a water spritzer handy. Serve shrimp at once with lemon wedges.

GRILLED SCALLOPS IN BACON

Guests eat as many of these as you can cook when passed as appetizers, and they are great for a quickly improvised dinner.

2 pounds sea scallops
2 tablespoons oil
2 tablespoons lemon juice
1/4 teaspoon white pepper
About 1/2 pound sliced bacon
Lemon wedges

Makes
6 to 8
main-dish
servings.

In a bowl combine scallops with oil, lemon juice, and pepper. Mix well, cover, and marinate at room temperature 30 minutes to 1 hour, turning once or twice. Cut bacon slices lengthwise in half, then crosswise, making 4 pieces of each slice of bacon. You will need a piece for each scallop. Remove scallops from marinade and wrap each in a piece of bacon. Spear with a wood pick soaked in water to prevent charring or thread 3 or 4 bacon-wrapped scallops on each short skewer, allowing space between for heat penetration. Scallops on short picks are more easily turned if placed in a hinged wire grill.

Grill 3 to 4 inches from hot coals for 5 to 7 minutes, turning as needed to cook evenly and prevent flare-ups. Serve at once with lemon wedges.

SAUCES AND SEASONINGS

Three distinct types of seasonings and sauces are used in barbecuing: dry seasonings rubbed on meats and poultry before grilling; marinades and basting sauces used on meats as well as poultry and fish before and during cooking; and table sauces brushed on meat just before the barbecue is done, then served as accompaniments.

Regional preferences for sauces have created virtual civil wars. If a map were colored to reflect shades of regional barbecue sauces, North and South Carolina would be amber colored (for their vinegar, butter, and hot pepper sauce); Georgia, orange-red (for its catsup sauce containing onion and vinegar); Florida, a more golden red (for its vinegar, lime juice, catsup, and horseradish sauce); with the colors darkening into catsup color as the eye moves toward Texas.

Sample the sauce recipes and choose those that suit your tastes. You will have a high adventure in cooking if you don't let regional prejudices hold you to one type of flavor. Ribs gain a pure, porky fresh taste brushed with a butter and vinegar sauce, North Carolina–style, then another evening they'll take on a ruggedly fragrant flavor, basted with a Mississippi-style or Tex-style sauce.

RIB SEASONING MIX

*T**his dry seasoning is rubbed into any cut of pork before barbecuing, and
sometimes it is used on beef.***

1 tablespoon salt

1 tablespoon sugar

1 teaspoon grated lemon peel

1 teaspoon monosodium glutamate (optional)

1 teaspoon freshly ground pepper

1 teaspoon paprika

*Makes
enough
for 10
to 12
pounds
meat.*

Mix all ingredients. Store in a small jar. Rub or sprinkle on ribs or
other pork (or beef) before grilling.

POULTRY SEASONING MIX

1 tablespoon salt

2 teaspoons freshly ground pepper

1 teaspoon monosodium glutamate (optional)

1 teaspoon paprika

1 teaspoon dry mustard

3 bay leaves, finely crumbled and stems removed

1 clove garlic, minced

*Makes
enough
for 6
to 8
pounds
chicken,
2 large
whole
turkeys.*

Combine all ingredients and mix together well. Store in a tightly
covered jar. Rub on chicken or other poultry before grilling.

BONE–BROTH BASTING SAUCE

Old-time chefs call beef broth bone-broth—too often overlooked as a meaty-flavored ingredient in a basting sauce—as for them it started with a good soup bone. This sauce can be used on beef or ribs. For lamb, make lamb broth of lamb stew meat and bones.

1 teaspoon salt
1 teaspoon dry mustard
1 bay leaf, finely crumbled
1 teaspoon chili powder, or to taste
½ teaspoon paprika
1 teaspoon hot pepper sauce
½ cup Worcestershire sauce
½ cup cider vinegar
3 cups beef broth, canned or homemade
⅓ cup oil
1 tablespoon soy sauce
1 clove garlic, crushed

Makes 4½ cups, enough to baste about 5 pounds meat.

In a stainless-steel or enamelware saucepan blend salt, mustard, bay leaf, chili powder, and paprika. Slowly stir in pepper and Worcestershire sauces to dissolve mustard, then stir in vinegar, beef broth, oil, soy sauce, and garlic. Bring to a boil. Let cool, pour into a jar, cover, and refrigerate overnight before using. Brush on beef, pork, or lamb for barbecuing. Leftover sauce takes on the smoky flavor of the meat, so some chefs think it even better the next time around. Refrigerate any leftover sauce and use within a few days or freeze.

CAROLINA BASTING SAUCE

To Carolinians who may say this isn't the one true sauce, I say it is one of them. Sauces vary from household to household—with more vinegar, more or less pepper, or crushed red pepper instead of the native-grown pepper that is full of fire.

2 cups cider vinegar
2½ sticks (1¼ cups) margarine or butter
1 teaspoon salt
1 tablespoon lemon juice
1 to 2 datil (bird) peppers, minced, or ¼ teaspoon
    crushed dried red pepper flakes

Makes enough for 3 chickens or 5 to 6 pounds pork or beef.

In a saucepan combine vinegar, 2 sticks margarine or butter, and the salt. Heat slowly until melted. Add lemon juice and peppers or pepper flakes. Use as basting sauce for chicken or pork. When meat is almost done beat remaining margarine or butter into sauce and serve as a table sauce. Leftover sauce can be refrigerated and used next time you barbecue.

WESTERN BARBECUE SAUCE

Soy sauce provides flavor-mellowing smoothness to many of the barbecue sauces used in the West.

¼ cup soy sauce
¼ cup catsup
½ cup dry red wine
¼ cup olive oil
1 small onion, chopped
1 teaspoon chili powder
1 teaspoon freshly ground pepper
1 clove garlic, minced

Makes 1¼ cups, enough for 3 to 4 pounds meat.

In a stainless-steel or enamelware saucepan combine all ingredients. Mix well and bring to a boil. Keep warm and brush lightly on lamb or beef while grilling. Any leftover sauce can be served as a table sauce.

GEORGIA BARBECUE SAUCE

Barbecue sauces in Georgia, Alabama, and Louisiana usually are sweeter than the spicy vinegary sauces of the Carolinas. Deep Southerners put catsup in their sauces, too. In Georgia this sauce would be used on whole hogs or pork shoulder barbecued in pits, and it gives a lively tang to grill-barbecued pork, too.

1½ cups catsup

1 cup cider vinegar

⅔ cup oil

⅓ cup Worcestershire sauce

½ cup packed brown sugar

3 tablespoons prepared yellow mustard

2 cloves garlic, minced

1 lemon, halved

Makes about 3 cups.

In a saucepan combine catsup, vinegar, oil, Worcestershire sauce, brown sugar, mustard, and garlic. Squeeze lemon juice into sauce and add 1 of the lemon halves. Heat slowly about 10 minutes. Sauce does not have to reach the boil; the heating helps blend flavors. Use sparingly as a basting sauce for fresh pork, ham, or ribs. Serve extra sauce heated as a table sauce.

CORNELL BARBECUE SAUCE

When chicken barbecues were great community events, this was the favorite sauce in Ithaca, New York. The egg helps the sauce glaze the chicken. I like to add tarragon, herbes de Provence, or rosemary.

1 egg

1 cup oil

2 cups cider vinegar

1 teaspoon salt

1 tablespoon poultry seasoning or other herbs

½ teaspoon freshly ground pepper

Makes enough for 5 to 6 pounds chicken.

Beat egg in bowl, then beat in oil until well blended. Stir in vinegar, salt, seasoning of choice, and pepper. Use as basting sauce for chicken.

FLORIDA BARBECUE SAUCE

One weekend barbecue regular says this sauce originated in Jacksonville, but I've had it or one of its variations in Miami, Georgia, and Alabama on ribs, pork roasts, chicken, beef, and even fish and lobster tails. I think it too pungent for seafood, but it is fine on ribs and chicken.

4 sticks (2 cups) margarine or butter
1 cup cider vinegar
1 cup catsup
1 (5- or 6-ounce) jar prepared horseradish
Juice of 6 limes or lemons
1 teaspoon salt
1 tablespoon Worcestershire sauce
1 teaspoon hot pepper sauce

Makes enough for 3 to 4 quartered chickens or 10 pounds ribs.

In a medium stainless-steel or enamelware saucepan melt margarine or butter slowly. Add vinegar, catsup, horseradish, lime or lemon juice, salt, and Worcestershire and pepper sauces. Simmer uncovered 20 to 25 minutes to blend flavors. Use as basting sauce for pork, chicken, or other meats, and serve as a table sauce. Leftover sauce can be refrigerated and kept up to a week.

Note: If using this sauce for chicken, lemons are better than limes; limes, abundant in south Florida, give a pleasant tang to pork and other meats.

TEXAS BARBECUE SAUCE

This sauce is served at table, spooned over meat or to the side for dipping each bite in. It also can be mixed with shredded pork or beef to make sandwiches. Do not cook with it.

½ stick (¼ cup) butter
1 small onion, chopped
1 clove garlic, minced
3 ribs celery, finely chopped
1 cup catsup
½ cup cider vinegar
1½ cups water
¼ cup Worcestershire sauce
3 bay leaves
1 teaspoon freshly ground pepper
1 tablespoon chili powder, or to taste

Makes 2 cups.

In a large stainless-steel or enamelware saucepan melt the butter. Add onion, garlic, and celery. Cook and stir until onion is tender. Stir in catsup, vinegar, water, and Worcestershire sauce. Add bay leaves and pepper. Simmer uncovered 15 to 20 minutes, stirring now and then to prevent sticking. Stir a small amount of sauce into chili powder and blend well. Stir chili mixture into sauce. Remove bay leaves. Let stand at room temperature 1 hour or longer before serving. Leftover sauce can be refrigerated for several days.

LOUISIANA BARBECUE SAUCE

Brush this sauce on just during the last 10 minutes of grilling ribs, chicken, or beef, as it burns easily. The sauce then goes to the table to be spooned over the meat.

1 cup each olive and vegetable oils
4 large onions, finely chopped
1 large green pepper, seeded and diced
1 rib celery, finely chopped
1 (8-ounce can) tomato sauce
3/4 cup catsup
1 teaspoon prepared mustard, preferably Creole-style
1 tablespoon vinegar
3 to 4 drops liquid smoke (optional)

Makes 4½ cups, enough for 10 to 12 pounds meat.

In a large stainless-steel or enamelware saucepan heat the oils. Add onions, green pepper, and celery and cook until onions are lightly browned. Stir in tomato sauce, catsup, mustard, vinegar, and liquid smoke, if using. Simmer 10 to 15 minutes.

ORANGE PEEL BARBECUE SAUCE

Citrus grove workers often keep a couple of orange peels drying on a high shelf in the pantry. You can do this, too, if you save a peel cleaned of its pith and juice; when it becomes leathery it is ready to use. You can buy dried orange peel in Oriental food markets, too.

1 tablespoon slivered or grated dried orange peel
1/4 cup each catsup, soy sauce, and orange juice
1 tablespoon honey
2 tablespoons oil
1 teaspoon freshly ground pepper

Makes 1/3 cup, enough for lightly basting 1 broiler-fryer or 3 pounds pork ribs.

Combine all ingredients. Use as a marinade and basting sauce for pork, chicken, or beef.

ALL–PURPOSE WINE BARBECUE SAUCE

This recipe can be used for any kind of meat, poultry, or fish; choose the wine to make it match. Because it is sugarless and contains no tomato, this sauce is less likely to burn than some others.

¾ cup red, white, or rosé table wine, or brandy

½ cup red or white wine vinegar

½ cup olive oil

1 cup minced chives or scallion tops

1 cup minced parsley

2 or 3 cloves garlic, minced

1 teaspoon salt

1 teaspoon freshly ground pepper

1 tablespoon soy sauce

Makes about 2½ cups sauce, enough for 5 to 6 pounds ribs, chicken, or fish.

This sauce is best if prepared the day before using it. In a large glass jar or bowl mix all ingredients, cover tightly, and let stand overnight at room temperature. Use as a basting sauce for beef, pork, lamb, poultry, fish, or game. This sauce also can be used as a marinade before barbecuing. Any leftover sauce should be refrigerated, as meat drippings will have been mixed into it with the barbecue brush.

RAISINBERRY SAUCE

12 ounces (2¼ cups) golden raisins

2 cups orange juice

1 cup water

¼ cup lemon juice

1 cup sugar

12 ounces (3 cups) fresh or frozen cranberries

1 tablespoon grated orange peel

Makes about 4½ cups.

In a large saucepan combine raisins, orange juice, water, lemon juice, and sugar. Bring to a boil, stirring to dissolve sugar, turn heat low, and simmer 10 minutes. Add cranberries and boil 5 minutes or until berries start to pop. Add orange peel and simmer 5 minutes or until sauce is reduced to a syrupy consistency. Cool. Pour into a large jar, cover tightly, and refrigerate up to 1 month. This can be used as a table sauce with barbecued meat as well as with roast turkey and other meats or as a marinade for pork or poultry.

CLASSIC SOY MARINADE

This sauce perks up pork, beef, lamb, or poultry and can be used for conventional broiling and roasting. I put a flank steak in this sauce to marinate before I go to the office, and grill it when I get home.

½ cup soy sauce

¼ cup dry white wine

2 tablespoons brown sugar

3 or 4 thin slices fresh ginger root, or ½ teaspoon
    ground ginger

2 cloves garlic, minced

Makes enough for 3 to 4 pounds meat.

Combine all ingredients and mix well. Pour over meat and marinate at room temperature 30 minutes to 2 hours or in refrigerator overnight.

DILL–LEMON BASTING SAUCE

This is obviously for fish, but try it on chicken and lamb, too.

½ cup lemon juice

½ stick (¼ cup) butter

1 tablespoon chopped fresh dill, or 1 teaspoon dill weed

½ teaspoon salt

¼ teaspoon freshly ground pepper

Makes enough sauce for 3 to 4 pounds chicken or 2 to 3 pounds fish.

In a small saucepan combine lemon juice, butter, dill, salt, and pepper. Heat until bubbling. Cool to lukewarm before using. (Another way to make this is to soften the butter, then beat all the ingredients together to form a smooth cream flecked with dill.) Use this sauce sparingly, as the high proportion of butter makes a fire flare up. The sauce can be brushed on with a sprinkling of fresh dill.

TOMATO BARBECUE SAUCE

1 medium onion, chopped

1 clove garlic, minced

2 tablespoons oil

2 (14½-ounce) cans tomatoes

2 ribs celery, finely chopped

1 bay leaf

3 tablespoons brown sugar

1 tablespoon prepared mustard

1 teaspoon hot pepper sauce

1 teaspoon salt

½ cup cider vinegar

1 teaspoon allspice

½ teaspoon ground cloves

Makes 3 cups, enough for 3 to 4 quartered broiler-fryers or 5 to 6 pounds pork.

In a stainless-steel or enamelware saucepan cook onion and garlic in oil until tender but not browned. Stir in tomatoes, celery, bay leaf, brown sugar, mustard, pepper sauce, salt, vinegar, allspice, and cloves. Cut up tomatoes, snipping through sauce with scissors. Bring to a boil, mashing tomatoes against sides of pan to chop more. Simmer uncovered 30 minutes. Remove from heat and discard bay leaf. If smoother sauce is preferred, puree in blender or food processor, making sure top of container is tightly closed so no hot sauce can spatter out. Use to baste chicken or pork and as a table sauce.

LEMON BUTTER

1 stick (1/2 cup) butter, softened
1 teaspoon grated lemon peel
Juice of 1/2 lemon

Makes
4 to 6
servings.

Beat butter until fluffy. Gradually beat in lemon peel and juice.

ANCHOVY BUTTER

1 stick (1/2 cup) butter, softened
3 to 4 flat anchovy fillets
1/2 teaspoon lemon juice
Freshly ground pepper

Makes
4 to 6
servings.

Beat butter until fluffy. Mash anchovies and beat into butter. Season to taste with lemon juice and pepper. Serve at room temperature as sauce for grilled fish.

CAPER BUTTER

1 stick (1/2 cup) butter, softened
2 tablespoons capers, chopped if large
1 teaspoon caper juice
1/2 teaspoon lemon juice
Freshly ground pepper

Makes 4 to 6 servings.

In a small bowl beat butter until fluffy. Beat in capers, caper juice, lemon juice, and pepper to taste. Serve chilled or at room temperature with fish or pork.

SAGE BUTTER

1 stick (1/2 cup) butter, softened
2 tablespoons minced fresh or 1 teaspoon dried
　　sage leaves
1 tablespoon minced fresh parsley
Juice of 1/2 lemon
Salt and freshly ground pepper

Makes 4 to 6 servings.

In a small bowl combine butter, sage, and parsley. Beat until fluffy and well blended. Beat in lemon juice, salt, and pepper. Cover and chill 30 minutes. Drop spoonfuls onto grilled pork or turkey.

SHALLOT–PARSLEY BUTTER

2 tablespoons minced shallots
1 tablespoon minced fresh parsley, preferably flat-leaf
¼ cup dry white wine
1 stick (½ cup) butter, softened
Salt and freshly ground pepper

Makes 4 to 6 servings.

In a small skillet combine shallots, parsley, and wine. Bring to a boil and boil briskly until wine has almost evaporated. Watch carefully to prevent burning. Cool thoroughly. In a small bowl, beat butter until fluffy. Beat in the shallot-parsley mixture, salt, and pepper until well blended. Serve spoonfuls on grilled steaks, pork, or poultry.

GREEN BUTTER

1 stick (½ cup) butter, softened
¼ cup minced watercress
1 tablespoon minced fresh parsley
1 tablespoon minced scallion tops
Juice of ½ lemon
Salt and freshly ground pepper

Makes 4 to 6 servings.

In a small bowl combine butter, watercress, parsley, and scallion tops. Beat until fluffy and well blended. Beat in lemon juice, salt, and pepper. Cover and chill 30 minutes. Drop by spoonfuls onto grilled fish, poultry, or other meats.

JANE TRUMBULL'S TARTAR SAUCE

Jane Trumbull whipped up this unusually delicate sauce for fish when her husband, Steve, grilled Spanish mackerel.

1 stick (½ cup) butter
Juice of 2 large limes
About ⅓ cup mayonnaise
6 scallions with tops, minced

Makes about 1 cup, 6 to 8 servings.

In a small saucepan melt butter. Stir in lime juice and beat in mayonnaise to make a smooth sauce that just barely holds a mound when dropped from a spoon. Stir in scallions. Serve at room temperature with grilled or fried fish.

KETTLE FOODS

A beloved uncle introduced me to Brunswick stew when I was very young. When caring for me while my mother was ill, he took me to a political barbecue. To keep me occupied while he talked politics and probably because I was hungry, he bought me a bowlful of the heady-smelling stew. I'll never forget the delicious blend of meat and vegetable flavors, or the funny paper bowl and wooden spoon used for such outdoor events. Today they would be plastic. The paper bowls have disappeared, but Brunswick stew and other great kettle foods go right along with barbecue in America.

In Alabama, Georgia, the Carolinas,

and Virginia it is Brunswick stew; in Kentucky, burgoo; and in Texas, great kettles of beans accompany barbecued meat. In California they are chili beans. In the Cajun country of Louisiana, a stew of fresh vegetables called maque choux is served at almost any big family party, including barbecues; and family reunions or barbecues in north Florida or south Georgia bring forth the best recipes for chicken or shrimp pilau (pronounced *per-loo*, and if authentic, highly seasoned with tiny datil peppers).

The most unusual of kettle foods, swamp cabbage in the Florida piney lands, has almost disappeared. The cabbage palm is rarely cut, but if you see a truck carting off bulldozed palms to a dump, grab them to cook. For eating, there should be about six feet from the base of the trunk to where the bud springs from the palm. I've manufactured a combination of fresh green cabbage and canned hearts of palm that simulates the old-time kettle palm, but fresh palm is better.

This chapter also includes two great main events cooked in a kettle or skillet—barbecued beef that is ladled onto toasted buns and a fish fry. I prefer a wide deep skillet rather than a kettle for fish, but some outdoorsmen tote along Dutch ovens filled with suet on fishing trips. If they're lucky, they heat up the suet, add the fish and hushpuppies, and have themselves a fine meal on the creek bank.

BRUNSWICK STEW

There are as many versions of Brunswick stew as there are barbecue chefs. This recipe is adapted from a famous woman cook in our little hometown, Montevallo, Alabama. The lemon gives a unique flavor, and I have cut sugar, catsup, and other old-fashioned ideas from the formula.

3 pounds broiler-fryer legs, or 1 stewing chicken,
    3½ pounds
1 pound boneless lean pork, such as rib end or shoulder
6 cups water, or as needed
2 onions, coarsely chopped
1 cup sliced celery
3 medium potatoes, peeled and cubed
1 lemon, sliced and seeded, peel left on
¼ cup Worcestershire sauce
1 tablespoon prepared mustard
2 teaspoons salt, or to taste
1 (14½-ounce) can tomatoes, or 2 cups peeled and
    chopped fresh tomatoes
1½ pounds green baby lima beans, shelled,
    or 1 (10-ounce) package frozen
2 cups corn cut off cobs, or 1 (10-ounce) package
    frozen whole-kernel

Makes 10 to 12 side-dish servings, 6 to 8 servings as a main dish.

In a large kettle combine chicken and pork with water to barely cover. Cover kettle and simmer until chicken and pork are tender, 1 hour for broiler-fryer legs, 1½ to 2 hours for stewing chicken. Remove chicken from broth, discard skin and bones, and return meat to broth. Remove pork and cut in chunks. Return pork to stew. I prefer chicken and pork in recognizable pieces, but some people like the meat shredded for a fine-textured stew.

Add onions, celery, potatoes, lemon, Worcestershire sauce, mustard, and salt. Cover and simmer 15 minutes, until potatoes are almost tender. Add tomatoes, limas, and corn. Cover and simmer 15 minutes or until limas are tender. Remove lemon. Serve hot in large soup bowls over rice. Crackers sometimes are passed on the side.

KENTUCKY BURGOO

Kentuckians tell you that burgoo goes with barbecue, but in Louisville I've also had it for a Derby breakfast—along with country-smoked ham, grits soufflé, and hot biscuits.

1 stewing chicken, 3 to 3½ pounds

2 pounds beef shank

1 pound lamb or veal stew meat

4 quarts water

1 tablespoon salt, or to taste

1 teaspoon freshly ground black pepper

½ teaspoon cayenne pepper, or to taste

4 medium potatoes, peeled and cubed

1 large onion, diced

1 cup peeled and chopped carrots

½ cup minced fresh parsley

2 (14½-ounce) cans tomatoes, chopped

2 cups shelled baby lima beans, or 1 (10-ounce)
    package frozen

2 medium green peppers, seeded and chopped

3 cloves garlic, minced

1 pound okra, sliced

4 cups corn cut off cobs, or 2 (17-ounce) cans
    whole-kernel

Makes about 30 side-dish servings, 20 main-dish servings.

In a 9-quart or larger kettle combine chicken, beef, lamb or veal, water, 2 teaspoons salt, black and cayenne peppers. Cover and simmer 2 hours or until chicken and meat are very tender. Remove meats from broth. Remove and discard skin and bones from chicken and bone from beef and shred the meats. Return to broth. Add potatoes, onion, carrots, parsley, tomatoes, limas, green peppers, and garlic. Mix and bring to a boil, turn heat low, and simmer 1½ hours, stirring often to prevent sticking. Add okra and corn and simmer 20 to 30 minutes longer. Taste and add more salt and pepper, if needed. Add more cayenne, too, if not spicy enough; burgoo should be tangy, but not really hot. Serve in soup cups as a side dish to barbecued pork, mutton, lamb, chicken, or beef, or in soup plates as a supper main dish.

CHICKEN PILAU

In north Florida and south Georgia, pilau is traditional with barbecue, picnic, and family reunion food. Pilau is one of the many food contributions of the Minorcans, the earliest remaining settlers of St. Augustine, but the English settlers from Georgia and other latecomers have changed the pronunciation of pilau to **per-loo**. Most pilaus are made fiercely hot with the tiny local chile, the datil pepper.

1 tablespoon oil or chicken fat
2 medium onions, finely chopped
2 medium green peppers, seeded and finely chopped
3 ribs celery, finely chopped
2 pounds chicken thighs, or 1 broiler-fryer, cut up
5 cups chicken broth
1½ teaspoons salt, or to taste
½ teaspoon white pepper
1 jalapeño, datil (bird), or other hot pepper,
    seeded and minced
1½ cups long grain rice

Makes 10 to 12 side-dish servings, 6 to 8 main-dish servings.

If you have homemade chicken broth in the freezer, fat from the broth can be skimmed for use in cooking the vegetables for pilau. Heat oil or fat in a large kettle, add onions, green peppers, and celery. Cook, stirring now and then, until onions are tender and translucent. Add chicken, broth, salt, and white pepper. Cover and simmer until chicken is very tender, 35 to 40 minutes.

Remove chicken from broth, remove skin and bones, and return chicken to broth. Add hot pepper and rice. Stir once, cover, bring to a boil, turn heat very low, and cook until most of liquid is absorbed and rice is tender, about 20 minutes. If rice cooks dry before it is tender, add ¼ cup hot water. If rice is too wet when done, uncover and cook over high heat to evaporate some of the liquid. Stir rice with a fork. Serve hot.

KETTLE BARBECUED BEEF

This famous Texas dish appears at dinner parties, suppers for high school football teams, and almost everywhere in Texas. The first kettle brisket that I had was flavored with a half bottle of liquid smoke, too potent for my taste. But the men present raved about it. My taste is for a tablespoonful in this recipe, but let your taste be your guide.

1 point cut brisket, 2½ to 3 pounds

¾ cup bottled chili sauce

¼ cup packed brown sugar

2 tablespoons Worcestershire sauce

1 teaspoon hot pepper sauce, or to taste

1 (12-ounce) can beer

1 tablespoon liquid smoke, or to taste

Makes 5 or 6 large servings.

Place meat in a plastic bag. Combine chili sauce, brown sugar, Worcestershire and pepper sauces, beer, and liquid smoke. Stir until sugar is dissolved. Pour over meat. Close bag tightly; turn to coat meat well with sauce. Marinate at room temperature 2 hours or in refrigerator overnight.

Place meat and marinade in a Dutch oven or large deep skillet with cover. Cover tightly and bake at 300 degrees 3 to 4 hours, or simmer over very low heat, until meat comes apart in shreds. Turn onto platter and pull meat apart with a fork. Serve meat with sauce on rice or toasted buns with pinto beans on the side.

KETTLE BEEF BARBECUE ON BUNS

Kettle barbecue is made in enormous quantities for block parties and other large groups. This recipe is easily doubled or tripled if you have a huge kettle. Any leftovers freeze well to heat up for lunches or supper later.

1 pound lean ground beef

1 large onion, chopped

2 cloves garlic, minced

1 (6-ounce) can tomato paste

3 cups tomato juice

2 teaspoons to 2 tablespoons chili powder (some like
   it hot)

Salt to taste

2 teaspoons celery seed

1 tablespoon sugar

1 tablespoon Worcestershire sauce

1 tablespoon vinegar

Hot water as needed

1 (12-ounce) can corned beef, or 1 1/2 cups shredded
   freshly cooked corned beef

4 to 6 hamburger buns, split and toasted

Makes

4 to 6

servings.

In a heavy kettle sauté beef, onion, and garlic until meat loses its red color, breaking up with a fork to keep crumbly. Pour off excess fat, or siphon off with a bulb baster, and discard. Add tomato paste and juice, chili powder, a little salt, celery seed, sugar, Worcestershire sauce, and vinegar to meat mixture. Cover and simmer 1 hour, stirring from the bottom now and then to make sure mixture does not scorch. After about 30 minutes stir in 1 cup hot water or more if needed; sauce should have a stewlike consistency but not be watery. Shred corned beef with fork and stir into sauce. Taste and correct seasoning. Serve on buns. This is eaten with fork and knife.

FRIED FISH AND HUSHPUPPIES

Frying fish in the back yard takes the onus off this sort of cooking. Any smell that clings to draperies dissipates quickly outdoors and any grease spatters are washed away by rain, if they are even noticeable. In hot weather, this is the only sensible way to fry fish.

3 panfish or small fish fillets per person
Salt and freshly ground pepper
White corn meal, preferably water-ground
Oil, at least a 24-ounce bottle for fish for 6
Tallahassee Hushpuppies (page 175)
Lime or lemon wedges

Spread fish on an enamelware or plastic tray and sprinkle lightly with salt and heavily with pepper. Scatter corn meal over fish to coat well, turn fish, and repeat seasoning and coating. Have fire burned down to hot coals at one side of grill, with more coals at edge to poke into fire if needed for more heat.

Place skillet over hottest part of fire and pour in 1/2 inch oil. Heat until almost sizzling. Add fish in a single layer, being careful not to crowd it. Cook over medium-to-hot heat until lightly browned; turn and brown other side. Fish will not turn golden brown, only a pale tan-gold color. If browned, it probably is overcooked. As fish is cooked, remove to a tray lined with paper towels. Let drain while cooking remaining fish and hushpuppies. Add more oil as needed.

As the last batch of fish is fried, drop hushpuppies in. Poke fire to spread coals as you need a moderate heat for the little fried breads. Fry hushpuppies and drain on paper towels. Arrange fish and hushpuppies on plates and garnish with lime or lemon.

MAQUE CHOUX

Louisiana Cajuns are legendary party givers. This summer vegetable mix is served with the mountains of crawfish and other delectables that distinguish a Cajun feast. If you can't get Creole or other first-class fresh tomatoes, buy the best canned ones.

6 strips bacon

1 medium onion, chopped

1/2 small green pepper, chopped

4 Creole tomatoes, peeled and chopped, or

      1 (14 1/2-ounce) can tomatoes

10 ears very fresh corn, kernels cut off cobs

1 teaspoon salt

1 teaspoon freshly ground pepper, or to taste

Makes 6 to 8 servings.

In a large saucepan sauté bacon until crisp. Remove bacon, drain, and crumble. Cook onion and green pepper in bacon drippings until onion is tender but not browned. Add tomatoes and simmer uncovered 15 to 20 minutes, stirring to prevent sticking. Add corn, salt, and pepper to taste. Simmer 10 minutes, stirring once or twice. Sprinkle with crumbled bacon and serve hot with barbecued or fried fish.

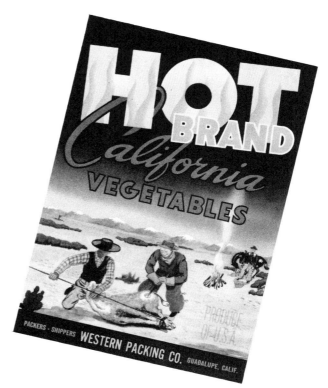

CALIFORNIA CHILI BEANS

Californians prefer pink beans to red or pinto beans and cook them with water, not tomatoes. The beans are seasoned lightly to modify the heat of spicy salsa or barbecued meat.

1 pound dried pink, pinto, or red kidney beans
Salt to taste
2 ounces salt pork, diced
1 large onion, diced
2 cloves garlic, minced
1 cup water, or 1 (8-ounce) can tomato sauce
1/2 teaspoon ground cumin
1 teaspoon chili powder, or to taste

Makes 10 to 12 side-dish servings, 6 to 8 as a main dish.

Soak beans overnight in water to cover generously. Drain. Place in a large saucepan or kettle, add fresh water, and bring to a boil. Turn heat low and simmer until beans are tender but not mushy, 1 1/2 to 2 hours. Check often and add boiling water to keep beans barely covered with water but not soupy. When almost tender, add 1 teaspoon salt. Meanwhile, in skillet, fry out salt pork. Add onion and garlic and cook until tender but not browned. Add water or tomato sauce, cumin, and chili powder. Simmer 10 minutes to blend flavors, then stir mixture into beans. Cover and simmer 20 minutes. Taste and add more salt, if needed. Serve as a side dish to barbecued beef, pork, or turkey or as a main dish with hot tortillas or cornbread.

Texas Chili Beans: Follow recipe for California Chili Beans, using pinto beans. Increase cumin to 1 teaspoon and chili powder to 3 or 4 teaspoons.

HEARTS OF PALM

In the Florida piney woods, this is called swamp cabbage. Sliced fresh hearts of palm, bacon, cream, and seasoning make up the classic recipe. I add fresh white cabbage to canned hearts of palm to produce a semblance of the old-time dish.

1/4 pound bacon or salt pork, diced

1/2 pound tender young cabbage, coarsely shredded

2 (8-ounce) cans hearts of palm, well drained

1/2 cup cream

Salt and freshly ground pepper to taste

1 pint shelled oysters (optional)

Makes 6 to 8 servings as a side dish, 3 to 4 as a main dish.

Fry out bacon or salt pork, add cabbage, and cook slowly until crisp-tender. Slice hearts of palm and add to cabbage. Bring to a boil in juices that are released from the vegetables. Add cream and simmer 2 or 3 minutes. Oysters can be added at this point and cooked just until the edges curl. Serve hot with barbecued pork, chicken, or fried fish.

GO-ALONGS

If you have skillets and saucepans for a grill, almost any vegetable or side dish that you serve indoors is possible with barbecue, but the popular accompaniments are grilled directly over the fire—grill-roasted corn, potatoes, or onions. The Clewiston barbecue in Florida shows how elaborate a simple barbecue can be. Clewiston lies on Lake Okeechobee, within a few miles of thousands of acres of winter vegetables. At a chicken barbecue, every vegetable available is served. Great kettles of water boil on the grill, ready to cook fresh sweet corn. One man assembles enormous platters of crisp vegetables—radishes, celery, carrots, cauliflower,

scallions, and winter tomatoes—to be dipped in a zesty sauce. Another makes huge bowls of coleslaw, using crates of new cabbage, scallions, and carrots.

Anything fresh and in season goes with barbecue. Those with summer gardens have a cornucopia of good things to serve with barbecue. Skewering enables you to grill zucchini, eggplant, and sweet peppers. And the best of all side dishes are coleslaw, mammoth salads of garden greens, and sliced tomatoes still warm from the summer sun.

Other accompaniments here include two kinds of hushpuppies, obligatory with ribs as well as fried fish in some parts of the country; chile cornbread, served with grilled steak in the Southwest and California; and green corn tamale, a summer favorite of Californians.

SKEWERED VEGETABLES

Eggplant, cut-up onions, zucchini, sweet peppers, and summer squash speared on skewers are ideal go-alongs to barbecued meats in late summer when the garden is at its peak.

Cut eggplant in large cubes or chunks or halve eggplants lengthwise to spear on skewers. The peel helps hold the vegetable secure on the skewer. Treat other vegetables simply; use good-size chunks of zucchini or other squash, peppers, and onions so they don't break off the skewers.

Brush the vegetables once or twice with the barbecue sauce being used for the meat or use a lightly herbed salad dressing or oil on the vegetables to prevent drying out. Since vegetables are being cooked with limited moistening, allow a longer cooking time if you insist on tenderness. Many barbecue fans like their squash still crunchy and eggplant before it is cooked to mush.

SPINACH AND TOMATOES

1 (10-ounce) package fresh spinach
2 tablespoons mayonnaise
Grated Parmesan cheese
1 tablespoon minced onion
Salt and freshly ground pepper
3 large tomatoes
Buttered bread crumbs

Makes 6 servings.

Wash spinach and cook in the water that clings to it until just tender, 3 to 4 minutes. Drain spinach well and chop fine. Mix spinach, mayonnaise, 2 tablespoons Parmesan cheese, onion, and salt and pepper to taste. Cut tomatoes in half crosswise. Place cut side up in a well-buttered skillet with heat-resistant handle or in a disposable foil pan. Spoon spinach mixture onto tomatoes; sprinkle with bread crumbs and more cheese. Place at edge of grill and heat thoroughly—about 30 minutes on an open grill, 15 to 20 minutes on a covered grill.

BABA GHANOUJ

This Middle Eastern spread is especially suitable for a barbecue appetizer, since charcoal-roasting the eggplant gives it authentic flavor. Roast and chill the eggplant the day before you plan to serve it, or serve it at room temperature.

1 large eggplant
Juice of 1 lemon
1 clove garlic, minced
Salt
1 tablespoon minced flat-leaf parsley
1 tablespoon olive oil
Pita bread, cut in quarters

Makes 4 to 6 appetizer servings.

Spear eggplant on a sturdy skewer or fork and grill 4 to 5 inches above hot coals until soft, about 25 minutes. Turn as needed to cook evenly. (Eggplant can be grilled over a gas flame or roasted in a moderate oven until soft, but the flavor will not have the traditional smoky tang.) Let eggplant cool until you can handle it.

Carefully peel and discard skin. Some of the pulp will stick to the skin, so scrape it off with a spoon. Place eggplant pulp in a bowl and squeeze lemon juice on it. Beat in garlic and salt to taste. Pile into a small serving dish. Sprinkle with parsley and drizzle with olive oil. Cover and chill until ready to serve. Surround with pita bread to be spread with baba ghanouj.

SKEWERED SUMMER SQUASH

The woodsy smoke brings out the best of summer squash flavor when it is brushed generously with olive oil and touched with garlic.

2 small yellow summer squash per person
2 cloves garlic, minced
1/2 cup olive oil
Salt and freshly ground pepper
Butter

Wash squash. Thread diagonally on skewers. (Squash can be cut if large, but they tend to cook to mush if the seedy sides are exposed.) Add garlic to oil and heat slightly.

Brush squash with oil and grill over moderately hot coals at edge of grill 15 to 20 minutes, turning and basting with garlic oil as needed. Serve with salt, a generous grind of pepper, and melted butter.

PEPPERED SUMMER SQUASH

2 tablespoons olive oil
2 teaspoons red wine vinegar
1/2 teaspoon freshly ground pepper
4 medium yellow summer squash
Butter, salt, and additional pepper

Makes 4 servings.

Pour oil and vinegar into a shallow bowl or pie plate, grind in 1/2 teaspoon pepper, then beat with a fork. Wash squash, split lengthwise, place in dressing bowl, and turn in the peppery dressing.

Grill cut side down over hot coals about 5 minutes or until tinged with brown. Turn, brush with remaining sauce, and grill until browned on skin side. Brush again with sauce and move to edge of grill to keep warm or serve at once with butter, salt, and more pepper. Total cooking time will be about 10 minutes.

ROASTED ONIONS

Sweet onions such as Vidalia onions from Georgia, Walla Walla onions from Washington State, Maui onions from Hawaii, and Hidalgo onions from Texas are wonderful cooked this way.

1 medium to large onion per person
Butter, salt, and freshly ground pepper

Pull off any loose skin from each onion but do not peel or cut. Wrap each onion in foil and seal tightly closed. Place over hot fire, 4 to 5 inches above coals. Roast until onions are tender when pierced with a fork, about 1 hour for medium to medium-large onions. Serve each person an onion still in its foil wrapper (it's not fair for the host or hostess to have to peel onions). Each person peels off the foil, splits or peels the onion, then butters it liberally and sprinkles it with salt and pepper.

ZUCCHINI OR EGGPLANT PARMESAN

1½ pounds zucchini or eggplant
2 tablespoons vinegar
1 clove garlic, minced
½ teaspoon salt
½ teaspoon freshly ground pepper
½ teaspoon paprika
⅓ cup olive oil
3 tablespoons grated Parmesan cheese

Makes 6 servings.

6/88
Very good

Scrub zucchini and cut in half lengthwise, or cut unpeeled eggplant in thick slices. Beat together vinegar, garlic, salt, pepper, paprika, and oil.

Place zucchini (cut side down) or eggplant pieces on grill 4 to 5 inches above hot coals, brush with oil mixture, and grill until tender, about 15 minutes, turning and basting as needed to cook evenly. Turn, brush again with dressing, and sprinkle with cheese. Grill until cheese is lightly toasted. Serve hot.

EGGPLANT STACKS

Each person is served a short stack of vegetables—eggplant is the base, topped with tomato and onion. The eggplant and tomato are tender and the flavors blended. The onion is still crispy. Cheese is softened atop the vegetable clumps for a saucelike topping.

1 clove garlic, peeled and split

1/2 cup olive oil

2 tablespoons dry red wine or wine vinegar

1 eggplant, about 1 1/2 pounds

2 tomatoes, about 1/3 pound each

1 small onion

3 slices Muenster or Monterey Jack cheese

Makes 6 servings.

Cook garlic in oil until it is golden. Remove garlic and cool oil slightly. Beat in wine or vinegar. Wash eggplant, but do not peel. Wash tomatoes and peel onion. Cut eggplant crosswise into thick slices. Slice tomatoes, making as many tomato as eggplant slices. Slice onion. Brush both sides of eggplant slices with the garlic oil. Place eggplant slices at edge of grill. Top each with a tomato slice, then an onion slice. Brush again with garlic oil dressing. Grill until heated through and tomatoes begin to moisten eggplant. Move eggplant stacks about with a spatula now and then to make sure they don't stick. Top with a half slice cheese each and grill until cheese is soft. Remove to platter and serve hot.

ONION STEAKS

Large sweet Spanish onions, the American-grown relative of the Bermuda onion and sometimes labeled Bermuda onions in markets, are ideal for this. The "steaks" will be the size of your outstretched palm.

2 large sweet Spanish onions, about 12 ounces each

Milk (fresh whole, skim, or buttermilk)

1 bay leaf, crumbled

About ½ cup flour

2 tablespoons oil

2 tablespoons butter

Salt and freshly ground pepper

Makes 6 servings.

Cut three ½-inch slices from the widest part of each onion, saving ends for other uses. Peel onion slices. Arrange in a shallow dish and almost cover with milk. Crumble bay leaf over onions and milk. Cover and refrigerate 3 to 4 hours, carefully turning onions once or twice. About 20 minutes before serving, remove onions from milk, handling carefully with a spatula so slices don't separate. (Milk can be saved for use in soup, sauces, or gravies.) Coat onions with flour. In a heavy skillet heat oil and butter over moderate heat at edge of grill. Cook onion "steaks" in hot fat until golden; turn and brown the other side. Season well with salt and pepper.

SWEET–SOUR ONIONS

This savory side dish to chicken, ribs, or burgers can be served hot, chilled, or at room temperature, a boon to the barbecue cook who can't coordinate fire and meat to a certain time.

4 medium onions, 1¼ pounds
1 tablespoon cider vinegar
1 tablespoon sugar
2 tablespoons catsup
½ teaspoon salt, or to taste
1 cup water
1½ teaspoons cornstarch

Makes 4 to 6 servings.

Peel and slice onions about ½ inch thick. Place in a 1½-quart stainless-steel or enamelware saucepan. Add vinegar, sugar, catsup, salt, and water. Water should about half cover onions. Cover pan and bring to a boil, turn heat low and simmer 20 minutes or until onions are crisp-tender. Add a small amount of water to cornstarch and stir to a smooth paste. Stir into onion mixture, cooking and stirring until smooth and translucent. Remove from heat. Serve at once, cool to room temperature, or chill before serving.

CREAMY GRITS

Don't feel ignorant if you aren't quite sure what grits is; just enjoy the discovery, as did my young friend who was busily cooking "big hominy," the swollen corn kernels that can be ground to make grits. Hominy grits comes in a package or bag and looks like fine chips of rice or dry corn. Properly cooked, grits makes a wonderful creamy-textured accompaniment to barbecued pork or game.

3 cups water

1/2 teaspoon salt, or to taste

3/4 cup grits (not quick-cooking)

1/2 cup cold milk

2 tablespoons butter

Makes 4 servings.

In a covered saucepan or top of a double boiler bring water to a boil. Add salt and stir in grits. Move saucepan to low heat or place double boiler top over boiling water. Cover and cook 15 minutes, stirring once or twice to keep smooth. Stir in cold milk, cover, and cook 5 minutes longer over direct heat or 10 to 15 minutes longer in double boiler. Stir in butter, cover, and cook 2 or 3 minutes longer. Serve hot with additional butter at table.

GARLIC GRITS ON THE GRILL

A *shortcut version of this dish, using packaged garlic cheese spread, is served by camp cooks with fried fish. I like this creamier grits dish, flavored with sharp Cheddar and a fresh clove garlic, with pork or game, as well as fish.*

3½ cups water

½ teaspoon salt, or to taste

¾ cup grits (not quick-cooking)

2 tablespoons butter

1 egg

2 ounces Cheddar cheese, coarsely shredded (to make
      ¼ cup)

1 clove garlic, peeled, smashed, and minced

Makes 4 servings.

In a heavy saucepan with tight-fitting cover bring water to a boil. Add salt and stir in grits. Cover and move pan to low heat. Cook, stirring now and then, until smooth and cooked to the consistency of very thick cream, about 15 minutes. Stir in butter and cook and stir until melted. In a small bowl beat egg and stir in a spoonful of the hot grits mixture. Stir the egg into the bubbling grits, cooking and stirring until well mixed. Stir in cheese and garlic, and cook and stir until cheese is melted into grits. Serve hot with additional butter.

GREEN CORN TAMALE

The farmland created by a flood control dam on the Los Angeles River about 15 miles west of city hall was planted in sweet corn when we lived nearby. Most of the crop was sold from streetside stands. Our Sunday afternoon ritual was to drive to Marie's Corn and wait in line for the freshly picked corn to be brought to the shed. Marie, a woman of vast wealth, it was rumored, operated the sales booth. Fieldmen harvested the corn and brought it to the stand minutes later. Marie and her daughter, their hands protected by heavy gloves, would pull a swath of shucks off each ear to check for kernel size and pest damage, then ask if you wanted small, medium, or large kernels. We chose small to grill in the husks and were mystified by our Mexican neighbors, who pre-ferred large kernels.

One Sunday, when I asked a man why he picked the larger, starchier kernels, he replied, "Green tamale." He explained how he made it, but only after several trials and some coaching by a friend who had inherited a recipe from an early governor of California did I master green corn tamale. This version works even in the oven of my New York apartment. The secret is to get a pasty dough that is not runny. I serve green corn tamale with steak, barbecued or broiled chicken, pork, or lamb, as well as with Mexican-style foods. The sweetness imparted by the corn husks produces a flavor unmatched by any other corn preparation that I've had.

The term green corn refers to fresh corn in green shucks, as compared to dried corn used for tortilla meal and the dried husks used for tamales when green corn is not in season.

10 ears mature green corn

1 teaspoon salt

1/2 stick (1/4 cup) butter, melted

1 cup corn meal, or as needed

1/2 pound Cheddar or Monterey Jack cheese, coarsely
    shredded

1 (4-ounce) can whole green chiles, drained and cut in
    strips

Makes 6 to 8 servings.

Shuck corn, reserving a dozen or so large husks. Wash husks and lay flat in a dish of water to keep moist. Remove silks from corn and cut corn off cobs deeply. A corn cutter can be used, but I stand each ear upright in a large shallow bowl and cut from top to bottom with a sharp knife. The corn can be chopped in a food processor, blender, or food grinder—or with a *metate*, a three-legged grinding stone that still is in use in the Southwest and Mexico. Grind the corn until it is doughy, though small pieces of fiber will remain. Season with salt and butter. Stir in enough corn meal to form a dough that holds its shape when pressed in the hand. If too crumbly, add more butter or a little water.

Line a well-greased 2-quart baking dish with corn husks, letting ends extend above rim. Spread a thin layer of the corn mixture over husks to anchor them. Sprinkle cheese over corn, then distribute chiles evenly in baking dish. Cover with remaining corn dough, fold husks over tamale, and press into top. Press additional husks into tamale. Preheat oven to 350 degrees and bake until firm but not dry, about 45 minutes. If top dries out before tamale is set, cover with foil. Serve hot with barbecued meat or beans.

GRILLED CORN

Corn cooked this way in view of the corn row makes every minute of time and energy put into a garden worth it. Harvest it just before you start the fire, and give the corn a half-hour soak in ice water to help it stay moist and tender while grilling it. It's hard to say how many eight ears of corn will serve. I've seen a mere boy eat four ears of corn cooked this way.

8 ears corn
Ice water in a clean pail
Butter, salt, and freshly ground pepper

Makes about 4 servings.

Pull back husks from corn and carefully remove silks. Push husks back in place and, if necessary, tie to hold husks firmly around corn. Soak corn in ice water at least 30 minutes.

Shake off excess water and place corn 4 to 6 inches above hot coals. Cook and turn to cook evenly until a test kernel spurts out juice when pierced with a knife point. This takes about 20 minutes. Serve immediately with butter, salt, and pepper.

CORN FOR A CROWD

A *separate grill for cooking corn when you are catering to a crowd simplifies traffic. The pot of water can be balanced in the center of the grill. Corn cooking works best as a team effort — one crew to husk and clean the corn, another to watch the boiling pot and cook the corn, and another to serve and clean up.*

You'll need a huge kettle. Fill it about 2/3 full and add 1 tablespoon sugar for each gallon of water (salt toughens corn; sugar accentuates the sweetness). Bring water to a boil. On a charcoal fire this may take up to a half hour. Add the freshly shucked corn an ear at a time, cover the pot, and bring again to a boil. Spread fire so heat dies to almost nothing and water ceases to boil. Let corn stand 6 to 7 minutes. Serve with butter, salt, and pepper.

Note: When passing corn outdoors, wrapping a half-dozen or so ears in a napkin or clean kitchen towel in a basket keeps it hot longer. The corn left in a large pot of hot water will hold for 20 or 30 minutes if the water is not allowed to boil again.

CHILE CORNBREAD

Quite typical of Texas and California, this cornbread must be baked in an oven. Serve it with a thick steak, cooked juicy rare, and an enormous bowl of green salad — a favorite summer evening combination in Hollywood. The cornbread is brought piping hot from the kitchen.

1/4 cup oil or bacon drippings

1 1/2 cups corn meal

1/2 cup flour

4 teaspoons baking powder

1/2 teaspoon salt

1 cup milk

2 eggs

1 (16-ounce) can cream-style corn

1 (4-ounce) can whole green chiles, seeded and cut
    in strips

1/4 pound Cheddar cheese, coarsely shredded

Makes 10 to 12 servings.

Preheat oven to 425 degrees. Add oil or drippings to a 9-inch skillet and while preheating the oven place pan in it to heat. A 9-inch-square baking pan also can be used.

In a bowl mix corn meal, flour, baking powder, and salt. Stir in milk and eggs. Remove pan from oven and pour oil into batter, leaving a heavy film of oil in pan. Mix batter well and pour half of it into hot pan. Spoon corn over batter, then arrange chiles over corn and sprinkle with cheese. Cover with remaining batter. Bake 25 minutes or until golden and done through. Center will be moist and custardy. Cut in wedges or squares and serve with butter.

CHILE–CORN CAKES

Chile-cheese cornbread is traditional with grilled steak in the Southwest. This version is crusty on the outside, soft as spoon bread in the interior, so it is eaten with a fork. A well-seasoned small black-iron skillet cooks it perfectly.

1/2 cup water-ground white corn meal

1/2 teaspoon salt

1 cup boiling water

1/4 cup cold milk

2 to 3 tablespoons oil

1/4 cup corn cut off the cob

1 1/2 ounces sharp Cheddar cheese, coarsely shredded
    (to make 1/3 cup)

1/2 to 1 canned green chiles, cut in strips

Makes 4 servings.

In a small bowl combine corn meal and salt. Add boiling water and stir until smooth. Let stand 15 to 20 minutes. Batter will thicken. Stir in cold milk to thin slightly.

Heat a 7-inch cast-iron or other heavy skillet thoroughly. Add 1 tablespoon oil and heat until sizzling. Add half the batter and tilt pan to let batter cover bottom of pan. Place pan over moderate heat and sprinkle corn cake with half the corn and cheese and arrange half the chiles on corn cake. Cook about 3 minutes, until underside is browned and firm. Carefully lift 1 edge of corn cake and fold over other half to form a half-moon shape. Cook 10 minutes longer, turning once or twice to brown well on both sides. Add oil to skillet, if needed. Remove corn cake to hot platter and keep warm. Cook remaining corn cake, adding more oil to skillet. Serve hot, cutting each half-moon in 2 portions. This crispy cornbread needs no additional butter.

TALLAHASSEE HUSHPUPPIES

Camp cooks, the story goes, fried corn cakes for the dogs, along with fish for the people, and tossed the cornbread to the dogs, saying, "Hush, puppy." A cook thought to taste a crispy nugget, and an American folk food was born. Hushpuppies go with fish, but are a barbecue regular, too.

1¾ cups white corn meal, preferably water-ground

¼ cup flour

2 teaspoons baking powder

1 teaspoon baking soda

1 teaspoon salt

½ teaspoon freshly ground pepper, or more to taste

1 large onion, finely chopped

1½ cups buttermilk or beer

2 eggs

Oil for frying

Makes 24 flat hush-puppies, 6 to 8 servings.

In a bowl combine corn meal, flour, baking powder, baking soda, salt, pepper, and onion. Stir in buttermilk or beer and eggs until well mixed. Hushpuppies customarily are fried in drippings from fried fish. You need ½ inch hot fish drippings or oil. Drop batter into hot oil by tablespoonfuls and cook until browned and puffed. Turn and brown the other side. Remove from fat and drain on paper towels. Continue cooking until all batter is used. Serve hot with fried fish, barbecue, or vegetables.

Note: These are light puffy corn cakes, not the hard doughy balls that are served as hushpuppies in most commercial places.

BISHOP'S HUSHPUPPIES

Bishop, a maintenance man at Texas A & M, has become a minor celebrity for his hushpuppies, spiced with three peppers and other seasonings. He and fellow workers periodically invite friends for a feast of catfish, beans, coleslaw, other Texas specialties, and the hushpuppies. Latecomers are in danger of missing out on the hushpuppies, so this is one party at which guests arrive on time.

1 cup each water-ground white corn meal and flour

2 teaspoons baking powder

1 teaspoon baking soda

1 teaspoon salt

1/2 teaspoon freshly ground pepper

1 medium yellow onion, finely chopped

4 scallions, including tops, finely chopped

1 or 2 jalapeño peppers, seeds removed, finely chopped

1 roasted and peeled fresh or canned sweet red pepper, chopped

1 1/2 cups buttermilk

2 eggs

Oil for frying

Makes about 24 flat hush-puppies, 6 to 8 servings.

In a large bowl combine corn meal, flour, baking powder, baking soda, salt, black pepper, onion, scallions, jalapeño, and red pepper. In another bowl, stir together buttermilk and eggs until well mixed. Stir into dry ingredients.

Pour 1/2 inch oil into a large heavy skillet and heat until almost sizzling. Drop batter into hot oil by tablespoonfuls and cook over moderate heat until browned and puffy; turn and brown other side. Remove from fat with a slotted spoon and drain on paper towels. Keep hot while frying remaining hushpuppies. Add more oil to skillet as needed to maintain 1/2-inch depth. Serve hushpuppies hot. They're especially good with fried catfish, barbecued pork, or vegetables.

VEGETABLE–BACON KEBABS

Cubes of eggplant, partially cooked carrot chunks, and mushrooms steamed slightly to prevent splitting can join these vegetables to grill on skewers.

2 yellow summer squash, about ¾ pound

2 zucchini, about ¾ pound in all

4 medium onions

4 large sweet red peppers

½ cup oil

¼ cup cider or wine vinegar

2 tablespoons minced fresh or 1 teaspoon dried basil

1 tablespoon minced fresh or ½ teaspoon dried thyme

2 tablespoons minced fresh parsley

6 to 8 slices bacon, cut in 1-inch pieces

Makes 6 to 8 servings.

Wash squash and zucchini and cut in 1-inch slices. Peel onions and cut into 4 wedges each. Seed and core peppers and cut in 12 squares each. Place vegetables in a plastic bag. Mix oil, vinegar, and herbs. Pour into bag, close bag tightly, and turn to coat vegetables well. Marinate at room temperature at least 2 hours. Thread vegetables on skewers, alternating types and placing a bacon piece between vegetables at intervals.

Grill 4 to 6 inches over hot coals 10 to 15 minutes, turning to cook evenly and brushing with marinade now and then.

COUNTRY–FRIED POTATOES

This simple old-fashioned food goes with almost any barbecued meat, and can be prepared at the edge of the grill with no special planning at all. I like the potatoes best when they are sliced and cooked unpeeled, but do as you please.

6 large thin-skinned potatoes, about 2 pounds

1 medium yellow onion, 2 to 3 ounces

3 tablespoons bacon or other meat drippings or oil

½ teaspoon salt

Freshly ground pepper

Makes 4 servings.

Peel potatoes or scour well with a brush under running water. Cut in ¼-inch slices. Peel and slice onion. In a large skillet heat drippings or oil. Add potatoes and onion and stir with a spatula to mix well. Cover and move to moderate heat. Cook about 10 minutes, watching to make sure potato and onion don't burn. Uncover, season with salt and pepper, and cook 10 to 15 minutes longer, until potatoes are tender and lightly browned.

Note: For variety, chopped green pepper, fresh green peas, snow peas, or thinly sliced carrot can be added to potatoes.

GRILLED POTATOES WITH CHEESE

4 baking potatoes, about 6 ounces each
1 large onion, sliced
¼ cup grated Parmesan cheese
4 teaspoons butter
Salt and freshly ground pepper

Makes 4
large
servings.

Peel potatoes and slice crosswise. Tear 4 squares heavy-duty foil and butter 1 side heavily. On buttered side of each square of foil pile a sliced potato, some onion, cheese, 1 teaspoon butter, and salt and pepper to taste. If potatoes look dry, add a tablespoon cream. Wrap foil packets loosely around potatoes and seal with a double fold. Grill over hot coals until potatoes are tender, about 30 minutes, turning packets to cook evenly. Turn out a packetful of potato onto each dinner plate.

GRILL–ROASTED WHITE OR SWEET POTATOES

1 potato per person
Oil (optional)
Butter, salt, and freshly ground pepper

Scrub potatoes. If soft skin is desired, oil skins well. For crisp skins, do not oil. Place potatoes over medium heat on grill and cook, turning every 15 minutes or so, until tender when pierced with a fork. Russets or other large white potatoes usually require 1 to 1½ hours; small potatoes, 45 minutes to 1 hour; and sweet potatoes, 45 minutes to 1 hour. Serve hot, slit skin in a cross and press potato to push up flesh through skin. Serve with lots of butter, salt, and pepper.

MY GRANDMOTHER'S POTATO SALAD

This basic potato salad is first-rate with barbecue, but you could add such things as sliced olives or pickle relish.

2½ pounds waxy potatoes, California potatoes, or other
    thin-skinned new potatoes
2 eggs
1 teaspoon Dijon-style mustard
2 tablespoons sherry, balsamic, or cider vinegar
3 tablespoons olive oil
2 large scallions with tops, thinly sliced
2 ribs celery, diced
½ cup mayonnaise
1 teaspoon celery seed
Salt and freshly ground pepper

Makes 6 to 8 servings.

Scrub potatoes and place in a large saucepan with enough water to barely cover. Cover pan, bring to a boil, and boil 10 minutes. Meanwhile, rinse eggs in hot water to warm them slightly to prevent cracking. Add eggs to potatoes and continue cooking until potatoes are barely tender. Eggs must cook at least 10 minutes. If potatoes are tender before they have cooked 10 minutes, lift out with slotted spoon. Cool potatoes just enough to handle and cool eggs promptly in cold water. Crack and shell eggs, pulling off membrane with shell. Wrap eggs individually in plastic wrap and refrigerate. Peel potatoes and cube them into a bowl.

In a small bowl stir together mustard and vinegar, then beat in olive oil. Pour over potatoes and toss to coat potatoes well. Cover and refrigerate 2 or 3 hours. To finish salad, add scallions, celery, mayonnaise to moisten, celery seed, and salt and pepper to taste. Toss gently but thoroughly. Turn into serving bowl and tuck crisp greens around the edges. Slice eggs and arrange in circle around outside of potato salad. Cover and refrigerate or serve at once.

BUTTERED POTATOES

A *French family was grilling these richly flavored potatoes on a tiny brazier when we picnicked near Avignon one spring Sunday. The family happily posed for a picture, pushing the smallest child front center to hide the grill and potatoes (the objects that we wanted on film), so we have a smiling little boy in our snapshot and no potatoes. We've grilled potatoes this way many times since.*

4 potatoes, about 4 ounces each
1 stick (½ cup) butter
Salt and freshly ground pepper

Makes
4 to 6
servings.

Peel potatoes, if desired, though I like the peel left on. Cut lengthwise in thick slabs. In a small saucepan melt butter at edge of grill. Brush potatoes with butter and place on grill 4 to 6 inches above hot coals. Grill, turning and basting with butter as needed to cook evenly and prevent flames, until potatoes are golden brown and tender, about 20 minutes' total cooking. Serve hot with remaining or more butter and salt and pepper.

BRANDIED MUSHROOMS

Flambé *these mushrooms for a dramatic accompaniment to a thick steak or burgers.*

½ stick (¼ cup) butter
1 tablespoon minced shallots or scallions
10 to 12 ounces fresh mushrooms, cleaned and sliced
Dash salt
¼ teaspoon freshly ground pepper
2 tablespoons brandy
½ cup heavy cream, or ¼ cup beef broth
    or dry red wine

Makes
4 to 6
servings.

In a skillet melt butter. Add shallots or scallions and sauté until aroma begins to deepen, 5 to 6 minutes. Add mushrooms and cook briefly, stirring gently once or twice. Add salt and pepper and stir once. Tip skillet so mushrooms and juices slide to one side of pan. Set pan straight and add brandy to dry side of pan. Immediately ignite. Stir in cream, broth, or wine as flame dies. Heat but do not boil. Serve with steak or thick hamburgers.

MUSHROOM WILD RICE

This is very special with beef, chicken, or turkey but some barbecue chefs serve it with anything from hot dogs to lamb.

1 stick (1/2 cup) butter
12 ounces fresh mushrooms, cleaned and sliced
11/2 cups wild rice
11/2 cups beef broth, or more as needed
11/2 cups mixed vegetable juice
Salt and freshly ground pepper

Makes 6 to 8 servings.

In a heavy Dutch oven melt butter. Add mushrooms and sauté until liquid that cooks from mushrooms is evaporated. Add wild rice and sauté, stirring occasionally, until well coated with butter and smelling lightly toasted. Add broth, vegetable juice, and salt and pepper to taste. Bring to a boil, cover, and simmer 11/2 hours, stirring now and then. If not ready to serve, add more beef broth, move to edge of grill, or turn oven heat very low and keep warm. The seasonings permeate the rice thoroughly when cooked this way and if made the day before, the dish can be reheated by adding a little hot broth.

FOUR PEPPERS SALAD

Anybody who finds a rainbow assortment of sweet peppers in late summer can serve this glorious salad. Specialty growers in our part of the country supply us and you can grow these fancy peppers from seed, if you are a gardener.

A large handful garden lettuce

1 each sweet green, red, yellow, and purple pepper

1 large scallion, sliced

6 to 8 cherry tomatoes, halved

About 3 tablespoons olive oil

About 1 tablespoon sherry vinegar

Salt and freshly ground pepper

Makes 6 to 8 servings.

Wash greens well, dry thoroughly, and tear into bite-size pieces into a salad bowl lined with paper towels to blot up stray drops of water. Discard towels, dumping greens back into bowl. Remove seeds and ribs from peppers, cut in rings, and arrange in separate piles over greens. Pile green onion in center and arrange tomatoes in another pile. Cover and chill until ready to serve. Bring salad to table before tossing.

Sprinkle with oil to moisten, toss gently, then add vinegar, salt, and pepper and toss lightly. Serve immediately.

ROASTED ORANGE HALVES

2 navel oranges

3 tablespoons melted butter or barbecue sauce

Makes 4 servings.

Place oranges in a large pot with water to cover. Bring to a boil and simmer until oranges are tender enough to be pierced easily with a skewer, about 25 minutes for medium oranges. Drain and cool oranges. Cut crosswise in half. Place skin side down at edge of grill and brush with melted butter or barbecue sauce (such as sauces with Smoky Ginger Duckling, page 105) and heat thoroughly. Brush again with sauce and turn cut side down. Grill until lightly browned and heated through. Serve—skin and all—with pork or poultry.

TEXAS COLESLAW

No salad goes with barbecued ribs as well as coleslaw, and I serve it with almost any barbecue.

1 pound firm white cabbage
½ small onion
2 tablespoons sweet pickle relish
¼ cup mayonnaise, or to taste
Salt to taste

Makes 4 to 6 servings.

Cut cabbage in wedges and cut out core. Peel onion and cut in wedges. Cut cabbage and onion on slicing blade of processor or shred coarsely. In bowl combine with pickle relish and mayonnaise to moisten well. Taste and add salt, if needed. Pickle relish provides enough sweetness for me. If you like sweeter coleslaw, add sugar to taste. Cover coleslaw and refrigerate until ready to serve.

FRESH CUCUMBER RELISH

2 cucumbers
½ small onion
1 teaspoon salt
1 tablespoon minced fresh dill, or ½ teaspoon dill weed
3 to 4 tablespoons cider vinegar

Makes 2 cups or 6 to 8 relish servings.

If cucumbers are waxed, scour with a brush and tepid suds made with dishwashing liquid detergent; rinse thoroughly and dry. Peel off bands of green skin so that about half the green portion remains to tint relish pale green. In a food processor or on a hand shredder, coarsely shred cucumbers and onion. In an enamelware, stainless-steel, or plastic colander, combine cucumbers, onion, and salt. Let stand in sink 15 minutes. Press out as much liquid as possible. Turn relish into bowl; stir in dill and vinegar. Cover and refrigerate until ready to serve.

SANTA MARIA SALSA

This is one version of the Cal-Mex cold tomato relish that goes with bar-becue and other foods eaten outdoors and at formal dining tables. It goes with steak, beans, lamb, chicken, or turkey on the barbecue table.

2 (14½-ounce) cans tomatoes, or 3½ cups chopped
    peeled fresh tomatoes
½ cup chopped celery
¾ cup chopped onion
¼ cup chopped green pepper
1½ teaspoons salt
1 teaspoon prepared horseradish
1 tablespoon vinegar
1 tablespoon sugar
1 tablespoon Worcestershire sauce
1 pickled jalapeño, minced, or to taste

Makes about 4 cups.

Finely chop canned tomatoes with scissors and mix with other ingredients. Turn into a bowl or jar, cover tightly, and refrigerate several hours or overnight to blend flavors. Serve at room temperature as a side dish with meats, beans, and barbecue. Any leftovers can be refrigerated for several days.

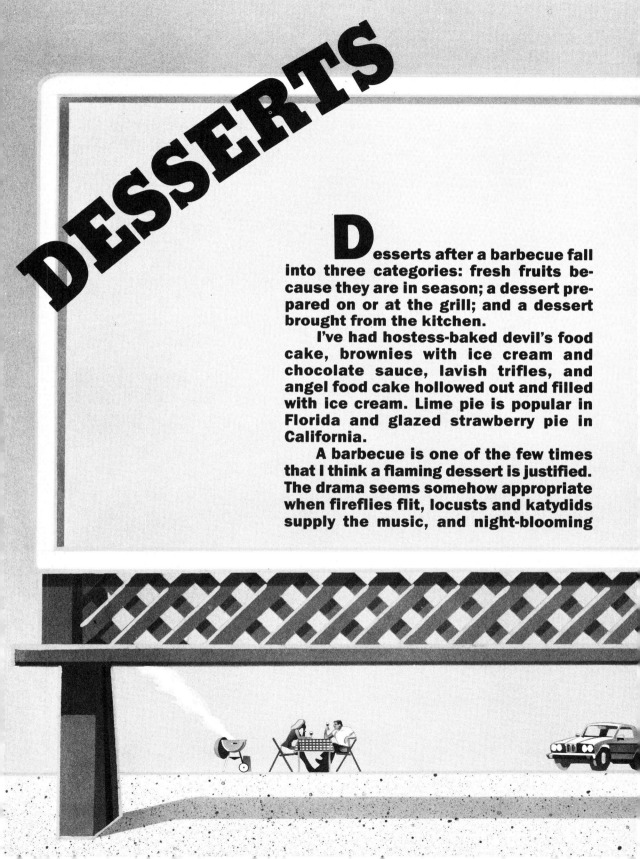

DESSERTS

Desserts after a barbecue fall into three categories: fresh fruits because they are in season; a dessert prepared on or at the grill; and a dessert brought from the kitchen.

I've had hostess-baked devil's food cake, brownies with ice cream and chocolate sauce, lavish trifles, and angel food cake hollowed out and filled with ice cream. Lime pie is popular in Florida and glazed strawberry pie in California.

A barbecue is one of the few times that I think a flaming dessert is justified. The drama seems somehow appropriate when fireflies flit, locusts and katydids supply the music, and night-blooming blossoms scent the air. Almost any fruit can be glazed in a skillet in butter and sugar, then flamed with a high-proof spirit.

But the only dessert you really need is a selection of good cheeses and a choice of summer's finest fruits—peaches, plums, Bartlett pears, grapes, cherries, or berries. Bring on the coffee and a good port or dessert madeira—what a way to end a day!

PEACH–BLACKBERRY COMPOTE

Raspberries or blueberries can be used instead of the blackberries, but blackberries seem extra summery and are increasingly available in big city markets.

2 cups water
1 cup sugar
1 vanilla bean
2 teaspoons lemon juice
5 to 6 peaches, peeled and sliced
1½ cups blackberries, washed and drained
1 cup heavy cream

Makes 4 to 6 servings.

In a saucepan combine water and sugar and bring to a boil. Split the vanilla bean, scrape out the seeds, and add remaining bean to syrup. Simmer the syrup 15 minutes, until slightly thickened. Remove from heat and stir in lemon juice. Cool slightly. Add peaches to hot syrup, cover, and chill 2 or 3 hours. Spoon peaches and some of the syrup into each dessert dish. Scatter blackberries over the top and serve with cream.

PEACHES IN PORT

If you tire of fresh juicy peaches during barbecue season, this is a refreshing alternative.

6 peaches
2 tablespoons butter
1 tablespoon sugar, or to taste
¼ cup port

Makes 6 servings.

Peel and slice peaches. (If not using at once, cover with water with juice of half a lemon in it. Just before cooking, drain peaches.) Melt butter in a skillet. Add peaches and sugar; cook and turn until peaches are coated with butter mixture. Add port and cook until sauce takes on a syrupy consistency. Serve warm with ice cream, sour cream, or whipped cream.

PEACHES WITH BUTTERED ALMONDS

This can be cooked in the kitchen and served outdoors or cooked at the edge of the grill.

½ stick (¼ cup) butter

¼ cup sliced almonds

2 tablespoons fine dry bread crumbs

2 tablespoons brown sugar

6 firm-ripe peaches

2 tablespoons water

2 to 3 tablespoons granulated sugar

2 teaspoons lemon juice

Makes 6 servings.

Several hours before serving, in a small skillet melt 2 tablespoons of the butter. Add almonds and bread crumbs and stir over moderate heat until lightly toasted and saturated with butter. Stir in brown sugar. Cool.

About 45 minutes before serving, in an 8- or 9-inch skillet heat remaining butter. Peel and slice peaches into hot butter. Cook a minute or 2 over moderate heat, add water, and sprinkle with sugar and lemon juice. Cook, stirring carefully so as not to break up peaches, just until fruit is tender. Spoon into dessert bowls and sprinkle with almond butter. Serve with cream or ice cream, if desired.

PEARS POACHED IN VANILLA SYRUP

2 cups water

1⅓ cups sugar

2 teaspoons vanilla extract

6 firm-ripe pears

Brandy custard sauce or whipped cream (see Note)

Makes 6 servings.

In a wide saucepan combine water and sugar. (The poaching syrup should be at least 2 inches deep; double the syrup ingredients, if necessary.) Bring to a boil, stirring until sugar is dissolved, and turn heat low. Peel pears and cut out blossom ends, but do not core. The core helps pear hold its shape. Carefully place pears in syrup and cook, turning with tongs to coat with syrup, until barely tender, 10 to 15 minutes. Lift from syrup and stand upright in a serving dish. After all pears are cooked, turn heat high and boil down syrup until slightly thickened. Pour over pears. Serve warm or cooled with custard or whipped cream.

Note: Make the sauce for these pears using a favorite recipe for soft custard flavored with Cognac or pear brandy, or by whipping some cream and folding in sugar and brandy to taste.

BUTTERED PEARS

In New York, the first Bartletts come to market in mid-July, so I can serve them for dessert several times before the barbecuing season fades.

4 large, firm-ripe Bartlett pears

3 tablespoons butter

3 tablespoons brown sugar

Vanilla or butter pecan ice cream

Makes 4 large or 8 small servings.

Peel and slice pears crosswise, removing cores and stringy fiber at center. In a 9- or 10-inch skillet heat butter and sugar. Add pears and stir gently to coat with butter and sugar. Cook, turning occasionally, until pears are tender but not mushy. Serve warm or reheat to serve. Spoon pears into dessert bowls and top each serving with ice cream.

FLAMING BANANAS

Sliced oranges, peaches, pears, or fresh berries can be flamed as well as bananas. Cook the soft fruit only a minute or two and flame with a matching liqueur or brandy.

6 firm-ripe bananas
½ stick (¼ cup) butter
2 tablespoons brown sugar
2 teaspoons lime juice
2 tablespoons dark rum, warmed

Makes 6 to 8 servings.

Peel bananas and cut into 4 pieces each, first lengthwise, then crosswise. In a skillet melt butter. Add bananas and turn in butter to coat well. Sprinkle with brown sugar and lime juice. Simmer 5 minutes, turning bananas once or twice to cook evenly. Place at edge of grill to keep warm. Just before serving, heat until sizzling and push bananas to side of pan. Pour in rum and ignite immediately at dry side of pan. Serve flaming on dessert plates with ice cream, if desired.

APPLES BAKED ON A GRILL

Baking apples (Rome Beauty, Jonathan, Greening, or
    Granny Smith)
Butter
Brown sugar or honey
Ground cinnamon
Freshly grated nutmeg
Chopped walnuts

For each person, tear off a square of heavy-duty foil large enough to wrap an apple. Core baking apples. Place an apple on each square of foil and fill core cavity with a pat of butter, a tablespoonful of brown sugar or honey, a sprinkle of cinnamon and pinch of nutmeg, and a few chopped nuts. Pull foil up around apple and twist closed to seal packet.

Cook apples at edge of grill, turning as needed to cook evenly. Apples will be tender in 35 to 45 minutes on a covered grill, in up to 1 hour on a brazier. Unwrap each apple over a dessert bowl and pour juices into bowl with apple. Serve warm with cream or milk, if desired.

TOASTED MARSHMALLOW SUNDAES

This is an adult dessert, so if children come to the barbecue substitute chocolate or butterscotch sauce for the liqueur.

6 dessert glasses of ice cream
Tia Maria or other coffee-flavored liqueur
6 marshmallows

Makes 6 servings.

Place ice cream in glasses on a tray and pour a big spoonful of liqueur over each serving so that it drizzles down slowly. Meanwhile, let each person toast his marshmallow over hot coals until golden and smelling of lightly burnt sugar. Slip marshmallow off the fork onto a dish of ice cream and eat.

ROASTED CHESTNUTS

Roasted chestnuts and crisp fall apples or pears make a splendid dessert for a fall barbecue on a weekend when the sunshine cooperates.

Fresh chestnuts in the shell, 12 per person
Corn or other vegetable oil

Peel a thin strip off the flat side of each chestnut, using a sharp paring knife. Toss chestnuts with oil. Place in a shallow pan, long-handled corn popper, or on a double sheet of heavy-duty foil pierced in several places to allow heat to circulate.

Place on grill about 4 inches above hot coals. Roast until shells pull away from nuts and a nutty aroma fills the air. Cool chestnuts just enough to be handled and let each person shell his or her own. The membrane must be peeled off the nut. Provide plenty of paper napkins for handling the chestnuts and wiping oily fingers.

A NOTE ON THE TYPE

The text of this book was set on the Linotype in Century Expanded, a type designed in 1894 by Linn Boyd Benton (1844–1932). Benton cut Century Expanded in response to a request by Theodore L. De Vinne for an attractive, easy-to-read type face to fit the narrow columns of his <u>Century Magazine</u>. Early in the 1900s Benton's son, Morris Fuller Benton, updated and improved Century in several versions for his father's American Type Founders Company. Century remains the only American type face cut before 1910 that is still widely in use today.

Composed by Superior Type, Champaign, Illinois
Printed and bound by Murray Printing Company, Westford, Massachusetts
Design by Stephanie Tevonian/Works
Concept consultant Keith Godard/Works
Billboard panorama illustrations by Dennis Ziemienski